CUP   PRINCETON

In Memory Of
ELDOR R. LEHFELDT

Donated By

HEATHER & SCOTT PEDERSEN

THE SURPRISING ADVENTURES OF THE MAGICAL MONARCH OF MO AND HIS PEOPLE

L. FRANK BAUM

1st WORLD
LIBRARY
Literary Society

The Surprising Adventures of the Magical Monarch of Mo and His People

L. Frank Baum

© 1st World Library, 2006
PO Box 2211
Fairfield, IA 52556
www.1stworldlibrary.com
First Edition

LCCN: 2006938086

Softcover ISBN: 978-1-4218-3381-1
Hardcover ISBN: 978-1-4218-3281-4
eBook ISBN: 978-1-4218-3481-8

Purchase *"The Surprising Adventures of the Magical Monarch of Mo and His People"*
as a traditional bound book at:
www.1stWorldLibrary.com/purchase.asp?ISBN=978-1-4218-3381-1

1st World Library is a literary, educational organization dedicated to:

- Creating a free internet library of downloadable ebooks

- Hosting writing competitions and offering book publishing scholarships.

Interested in more 1st World Library books?
contact: literacy@1stworldlibrary.com
Check us out at: www.1stworldlibrary.com

1st World Library Literary Society

Giving Back to the World

"If you want to work on the core problem, it's early school literacy."

- James Barksdale, former CEO of Netscape

"No skill is more crucial to the future of a child, or to a democratic and prosperous society, than literacy."

- Los Angeles Times

Literacy... means far more than learning how to read and write... The aim is to transmit... knowledge and promote social participation."

- UNESCO

"Literacy is not a luxury, it is a right and a responsibility. If our world is to meet the challenges of the twenty-first century we must harness the energy and creativity of all our citizens."

- President Bill Clinton

"Parents should be encouraged to read to their children, and teachers should be equipped with all available techniques for teaching literacy, so the varying needs and capacities of individual kids can be taken into account."

- Hugh Mackay

To the Comrade of my boyhood days

Dr. Henry Clay Baum

TO THE READER

This book has been written for children. I have no shame in acknowledging that I, who wrote it, am also a child; for since I can remember my eyes have always grown big at tales of the marvelous, and my heart is still accustomed to go pit-a-pat when I read of impossible adventures. It is the nature of children to scorn realities, which crowd into their lives all too quickly with advancing years. Childhood is the time for fables, for dreams, for joy.

These stories are not true; they could no be true and be so marvelous. No one is expected to believe them; they were meant to excite laughter and to gladden the heart.

Perhaps some of those big, grown-up people will poke fun of us—at you for reading these nonsense tales of the Magical Monarch, and at me for writing them. Never mind. Many of the big folk are still children—even as you and I. We cannot measure a child by a standard of size or age. The big folk who are children will be our comrades; the others we need not consider at all, for they are self-exiled from our domain.

L. FRANK BAUM.

June, 1903.

CONTENTS

THE FIRST SURPRISE

THE BEAUTIFUL VALLEY OF MO

I dare say there are several questions you would like to ask at the very beginning of this history. First: Who is the Monarch of Mo? And why is he called the Magical Monarch? And where *is* Mo, anyhow? And why have you never heard of it before? And can it be reached by a railroad or a trolley-car, or must one walk all the way?

These questions I realize should be answered before we (that "we" means you and the book) can settle down for a comfortable reading of all the wonders and astonishing adventures I shall endeavor faithfully to relate.

In the first place, the Monarch of Mo is a very pleasant personage holding the rank of King. He is not very tall, nor is he very short; he is midway between fat and lean; he is delightfully jolly when he is not sad, and seldom sad if he can possibly be jolly. How old he may be I have never dared to inquire; but when we realize that he is destined to live as long as the Valley of Mo exists we may reasonably suppose the Monarch of Mo is exactly as old as his native land. And no one in Mo has ever reckoned up the years to see how many they have been. So we will just say that the Monarch of Mo and the Valley of Mo are each a part of the other, and can not be separated.

He is not called the Magical Monarch because he deals in

magic—for he doesn't deal in magic. But he leads such a queer life in such a queer country that his history will surely seem magical to us who inhabit the civilized places of the world and think that anything we can not find a reason for must be due to magic. The life of the Monarch of Mo seems simple enough to him, you may be sure, for he knows no other existence. And our ways of living, could he know of them, would doubtless astonish him greatly.

The land of Mo, which is ruled by the King we call the Magical Monarch, is often spoken of as the "Beautiful Valley." If they would only put it on the maps of our geographies and paint it pink or light green, and print a big round dot where the King's castle stands, it would be easy enough to point out to you its exact location. But I can not find the Valley of Mo in any geography I have examined; so I suspect the men who made these instructive books really know nothing about Mo, else it would surely be on the maps.

Of one thing I am certain: that no other country included in the maps is so altogether delightful as the Beautiful Valley of Mo.

The sun shines all the time, and its rays are perfumed. The people who live in the Valley do not sleep, because there is no night. Everything they can possibly need grows on the trees, so they have no use for money at all, and that saves them a deal of worry.

There are no poor people in this quaint Valley. When a person desires a new hat he waits till one is ripe, and then picks it and wears it without asking anybody's permission. If a lady wishes a new ring, she examines carefully those upon the ring-tree, and when she finds one that fits her finger she picks it and wears it upon her hand. In this way they procure all they desire.

There are two rivers in the Land of Mo, one of which flows milk of a very rich quality. Some of the islands in Milk River are made of excellent cheese, and the people are welcome to spade up this cheese whenever they wish to eat it. In the little pools near the bank, where the current does not flow swiftly, delicious cream rises to the top of the milk, and instead of water-lilies great strawberry leaves grow upon the surface, and the ripe, red berries lie dipping their noses into the cream, as if inviting you to come and eat them. The sand that forms the river bank is pure white sugar, and all kinds of candies and bonbons grow thick on the low bushes, so that any one may pluck them easily.

These are only a few of the remarkable things that exist in the Beautiful Valley.

The people are merry, light-hearted folk, who live in beautiful houses of pure crystal, where they can rest themselves and play their games and go in when it rains. For it rains in Mo as it does everywhere else, only it rains lemonade; and the lightning in the sky resembles the most beautiful fireworks; and the thunder is usually a chorus from the opera of Tannhauser.

No one ever dies in this Valley, and the people are always young and beautiful. There is the King and a Queen, besides several princes and princesses. But it is not much use being a prince in Mo, because the King can not die; therefore a prince is a prince to the end of his days, and his days never end.

Strange things occur in this strange land, as you may imagine; and while I relate some of these you will learn more of the peculiar features of the Beautiful Valley.

THE SECOND SURPRISE

THE STRANGE ADVENTURES OF THE KING'S HEAD

A good many years ago, the Magical Monarch of Mo became annoyed by the Purple Dragon, which came down from the mountains and ate up a patch of his best chocolate caramels just as they were getting ripe.

So the King went out to the sword-tree and picked a long, sharp sword, and tied it to his belt and went away to the mountains to fight the Purple Dragon.

The people all applauded him, saying one to another:

"Our King is a good King. He will destroy this naughty Purple Dragon and we shall be able to eat the caramels ourselves."

But the Dragon was not alone naughty; it was big, and fierce, and strong, and did not want to be destroyed at all.

Therefore the King had a terrible fight with the Purple Dragon and cut it with his sword in several places, so that the raspberry juice which ran in its veins squirted all over the ground.

It is always difficult to kill Dragons. They are by nature thick-skinned and tough, as doubtless every one has heard. Besides, you must not forget that this was a Purple Dragon, and all scientists who have studied deeply the character of Dragons say those of a purple color at the most disagreeable to fight with.

L. Frank Baum

So all the King's cutting and slashing had no effect upon the monster other than to make him angry. Forgetful of the respect due to a crowned King, the wicked Dragon presently opening wide its jaws and bit his Majesty's head clean off his body. Then he swallowed it.

Of course the King realized it was useless to continue to fight after that, for he could not see where the Dragon was. So he turned and tried to find his way back to his people. But at every other step he would bump into a tree, which made the naughty Dragon laugh at him. Furthermore, he could not tell in which direction he was going, which is an unpleasant feeling under any circumstances.

At last some of the people came to see if the King had succeeded in destroying the Dragon, and found their monarch running around in a circle, bumping into trees and rocks, but not getting a step nearer home. SO they took his hand and led him back to the palace, where every one was filled with sorrow at the sad sight of the headless King. Indeed, his devoted subjects, for the first time in their lives, came as near to weeping as an inhabitant of the Valley of Mo can.

"Never mind," said the King, cheerfully; "I can get along very well without a head; and, as a matter of fact, the loss has its advantages. I shall not be obliged to brush my hair, or clean my teeth, or wash my ears. So do not grieve, I beg of you, but be happy and joyful as you were before." Which showed the King had a good heart; and, after all, a good heart is better than a head, any say.

The people, hearing him speak out of his neck (for he had no mouth), immediately began to laugh, which in a short time led to their being as happy as ever.

But the Queen was not contented.

"My love," she said to him, "I can not kiss you any more, and that will break my heart."

Thereupon the King sent word throughout the Valley that any one who could procure for him a new head should wed one of the princesses.

The princesses were all exceedingly pretty girls, and so it was not long before one man made a very nice head out of candy and brought it to the King. It did not look exactly like the old head, but the efface was very sweet, nevertheless; so the King put it on and the Queen kissed it at once with much satisfaction.

The young man had put a pair of glass eyes in the head, with which the King could see very well after he got used to them.

According to the royal promise, the young man was now called into the palace and asked to take his pick of the princesses. There were all so sweet and lady-like that he had some trouble in making a choice; but at last he took the biggest, thinking that he would thus secure the greatest reward, and they were married amid great rejoicing.

But, a few days afterward, the King was caught out in a rainstorm, and before he could get home his new head had melted in the great shower of lemonade that fell. Only the glass eyes were left, and these he put in his pocket and went sorrowfully to tell the Queen of his new misfortune.

Then another young man who wanted to marry a princess made the King a head out of dough, sticking in it the glass eyes; and the King tried it on and found that it fitted very well. So the young man was given the next biggest princess.

But the following day the sun chance to shine extremely hot, and when the King walked out it baked his dough head into bread, at which the monarch felt very light-headed. And when the birds saw the bread they flew down from the trees, perched upon the King's shoulder and quickly ate up his new head. All but the glass eyes.

L. Frank Baum

Again the good King was forced to go home to the Queen without a head, and the lady firmly declared that this time her husband must have a head warranted to last at least as long as the honeymoon of the young man who made it; which was not at all unreasonable under the circumstances.

So a request was sent to all loyal subjects throughout the Valley asking them to find a head for their King that was neat and substantial.

In the meantime the King had a rather hard time of it. When he wished to go any place he was obliged to hold out in front of him, between his thumbs and fingers, the glass eyes, that they might guide his footsteps. This, as you may imagine, made his Majesty look rather undignified, and dignity is very important to every royal personage.

At last a wood-chopper in the mountains made a head out of wood and sent it to the King. It was neatly carved, besides being solid and durable; moreover, it fitted the monarch's neck to the T. So the King rummaged in his pocket and found the glass eyes, and when these were put in the new head the King announced his satisfaction.

There was only one drawback—he couldn't smile, as the wooden face was too stiff; and it was funny to hear his Majesty laughing heartily while his face maintained a solemn expression. But the glass eyes twinkled merrily and every one knew that he was the same kind-hearted monarch of old, although he had become, of necessity, rather hard-headed.

Then the King sent word to the wood-chopper to come to the palace and take his pick of the princesses, and preparations were at once begun for the wedding.

But the wood-chopper, on his way to the court, unfortunately passed by the dwelling of the Purple Dragon and stopped to speak to the monster.

Now it seems that when the Dragon had swallowed the King's head, the unusual meal made the beast ill. It was more accustomed to berries and caramels for dinner than to heads, and the sharp points of the King's crown (which was firmly fastened to the head) pricked the Dragon's stomach and made the creature miserable. After a few days of suffering the Dragon disgorged the head, and, not knowing what else to do with it, locked it up in a cupboard and put the key in its pocket.

When the Dragon met the wood-chopper and learned he had made a new head for the King, and as a reward was to wed one of the princesses, the monster became very angry. It resolved to do a wicked thing; which will not surprise you when you remember the beast's purple color.

"Step into my parlor and rest yourself," said the Dragon, politely. Wicked people are most polite when they mean mischief.

"Thank you, I'll stop for a few minutes," replied the wood-chopper; "but I can not stay long, as I am expected at court."

When he had entered the parlor the Dragon suddenly opened its mouth and snapped off the poor wood-chopper's head. Being warned by experience, however, it did not swallow the head, but placed it in the cupboard. Then the Dragon took from a shelf the King's head and glued it on the wood-chopper's neck.

"Now," said the beast, with a cruel laugh, "you are the King! Go home and claim your wife and your kingdom."

The poor wood-chopper was much amazed; for at first he did not really know which he was, the King or the wood-chopper.

He looked in the mirror and, seeing the King, made a low bow. Then the King's head thought: "Who am I bowing to? There is no one greater than the King!" And so at once there began a conflict between the wood-chopper's heart and the

L. Frank Baum

King's head.

The Dragon was mightily pleased at the result of its wicked stratagem, and having pushed the bewildered wood-chopper out of the castle, immediately sent him on his way to the court.

When the poor man neared the town the people ran out and said: "Why, this is the King come back again. All hail, your Majesty!"

"All nonsense!" returned the wood-chopper. "I am only a poor man with the King's head on my shoulders. You can easily see it isn't mine, for it's crooked; the Dragon didn't glue it on straight."

"Where, then, is your own head?" they asked.

"Locked up in the Dragon's cupboard," replied the poor fellow, beginning to weep.

"Here," cried the King's head; "stop this. You mustn't cry out of my eyes! The King never weeps."

"I beg pardon, your Majesty," said the wood-chopper, meekly, "I'll not do it again."

"Well, see that you don't," returned the head more cheerfully.

The people were greatly amazed at this, and took the wood-chopper to the palace, where all was soon explained.

When the Queen saw the King's head she immediately kissed it; but the King rebuked her, saying she must kiss only him.

"But it is your head," said the poor Queen.

"Probably it is," replied the King; "but it is on another man. You must confine yourself to kissing my wooden head."

"I'm sorry," sighed the Queen, "for I like to kiss the real head best."

"And so you shall," said the King's head; "I don't approve your kissing that wooden head at all."

The poor lady looked from one to the other in perplexity. Finally a happy thought occurred to her.

"Why don't you trade heads?" she asked.

"Just the thing!" cried the King; and, the wood-chopper consenting, the exchange was made, and the Monarch of Mo found himself in possession of his own head again, whereat he was so greatly pleased that he laughed long and merrily.

The wood-chopper, however, did not even smile. He couldn't because of the wooden face. The head he had made for the King he now was compelled to wear himself.

"Bring hither the princesses," commanded the King. "This good man shall choose his bride at once, for he has restored to me my own head."

But when the princesses arrived and saw that the wood-chopper had a wooden head, they each and all refused to marry him, and begged so hard to escape that the King was in a quandary.

"I promised him one of my daughters," he argued, "and a King never breaks his word."

"But he hadn't a wooden head then," explained one of the girls.

The King realized the truth of this. Indeed, when he came to look carefully at the wooden head, he did not blame his daughters for not wishing to marry it. Should he force one of them to consent, it was not unlikely she would call her

L. Frank Baum

husband a blockhead—a term almost certain to cause trouble in any family.

After giving the matter deep thought, the King resolved to go to the Purple Dragon and oblige it to give up the wood-chopper's head.

So all the fighting men in the kingdom were got together, and, having picked ripe swords off the sword-trees, they marched in a great body to the Dragon's castle.

Now the Purple Dragon realized that if it attempted to fight all this army, it would perhaps be cut to pieces; so it retired within its castle and refused to come out.

The wood-chopper was a brave man.

"I'll go in and fight the Dragon alone," he said; and in he went. By this time the Dragon was both frightened and angry, and the moment it saw the man it rushed forward and made a snap at his head.

The wooden head came off at once, and the Dragon's long, sharp teeth got stuck in the wood and would not come out again; so the monster was unable to do anything but flop its tail and groan.

The wood-chopper now ran to the cupboard, took out his head and placed it upon his shoulders where it belonged. Then he proudly walked out of the castle and was greeted with loud shouts by the army, which carried him back in triumph to the King's palace.

And, now that he wore his own head again, one of the prettiest of the young princesses willingly agreed to marry him; so the wedding ceremony was performed amidst great rejoicing.

THE THIRD SURPRISE

THE TRAMP DOG AND
THE MONARCH'S LOST TEMPER

One day the Monarch of Mo, having nothing better to do, resolved to go hunting blackberries among the bushes that grew at the foot of the mountains.

So he put on an old crown that would not get tarnished if it rained, and, having found a tin pail in the pantry, started off without telling any one where he was going.

For some distance the path was a nice, smooth taffy, that was very agreeable to walk on; but as he got nearer the mountains the ground became gravelly, the stones being jackson-balls and gum-drops; so that his boots, which were a little green when he picked them, began to hurt his feet.

But the King was not easily discouraged, and kept on until he found the blackberry bushes, when he immediately began to fill his pail, the berries being remarkably big and sweet.

While thus occupied he heard a sound of footsteps coming down the mountain side, and presently a little dog ran out from the bushes and trotted up to him.

Now there were no dogs at all in Mo, and the King had never seen a creature like this before; therefore he was greatly surprised, and said:

"What are you, and where do you come from?"

The dog also was surprised at this question, and looked suspiciously at the King's tin pail; for many times wicked boys had tied such a pail to the end of his tail. In fact, that was the reason he had run away from home and found his way, by accident, to the Valley of Mo.

"My name is Prince," replied the gravely; "and I have come from a country beyond the mountains and the desert."

"Indeed! are you in truth a prince?" exclaimed the monarch; "then you will be welcome in my kingdom, where we always treat nobility with proper respect. But why do you have four feet?"

"Because six would be too many," replied the dog.

"But I have only two," said the King.

"I am sorry," said the dog, who was something of a wag, "because where I come from it is more fashionable to walk on four feet."

"I like to be in the fashion," remarked the King, thoughtfully; "but what am I to do, having only two legs?"

"Why, I suppose you could walk on your hands and feet," returned the dog with a laugh.

"So I will," said the King, being pleased with the idea; "and you shall come to the palace with me and teach me all the fashions of the country from whence you came."

The King got down on his hands and knees, and was delighted to find he could get along in this way very nicely.

"How am I to carry my pail?" he asked.

"In your mouth, of course," replied the dog. This suggestion seeming a happy one, the King took the pail in his mouth and they started back toward the palace. But when his Majesty came to the gum-drops and jackson-balls they hurt his hands and knees, so that he groaned aloud. But the dog only laughed. Finally they reached a place where it was quite muddy. Of course the mud was only jelly, but it hadn't dried up since the last rain. The dog jumped over the place nimbly enough, but when the King tried to do likewise he failed, and came down into the jelly with both hands and knees, and stuck fast.

Now the monarch had a very good temper, which he carried in his vest pocket; but as he passed over the gum-drop pebbles on his hands and knees this temper dropped out of his pocket, and, having lost it, he became very angry at the dog for getting him into such a scrape.

So he began to scold, and when he opened his mouth the pail dropped out and the berries were all spilled. This made the dog laugh more than ever, at which the King pulled himself out of the jelly, jumped to his feet, and began to chase the dog as fast as he could. Finally the dog climbed a tall tree where the King could not reach him, and when safe among the branches he looked down and said: "See how foolish a man becomes who tries to be in fashion rather than live as nature intended he should! You can no more be a dog than I can be a king; so hereafter, if you are wise, you will be content to walk on two legs."

"There is much truth in what you say," replied the Monarch of Mo. "Come with me to the palace, and you shall be forgiven; indeed, we shall have a fine feast in honor of your arrival."

So the dog climbed down from the tree and followed the King to the palace, where all the courtiers were astonished to see so queer an animal, and made a great favorite of him.

After dinner the King invited the dog to take a walk around the grounds of the royal mansion, and they started out merrily enough. But the King's boots had begun to hurt him again; for, as they did not fit, being picked green, they had rubbed his toes until he had corns on them. So when they reached the porch in front of the palace the King asked:

"My friend, what is good for corns?"

"Tight boots," replied the dog, laughing; "but they are not very good for your feet."

Now the King, not yet having found his lost temper, became exceedingly angry at this poor jest; so he rushed at the dog and gave it a tremendous kick.

Up into the air like a ball flew the dog, while the King, having hurt his toe by the kick, sat down on the door-step and nursed his foot while he watched the dog go farther and farther up, until it seemed like a tiny speck against the blue of the sky.

"I must have kicked harder than I thought," said the King, ruefully; "there he goes, out of sight, and I shall never see him again!"

He now limped away into the back garden, where he picked a new pair of boots that would not hurt his feet; and while he was gone the dog began to fall down again. Of course he fell faster than he went up, and finally landed with a crash exactly on the King's door-step. But so great was the force of the fall and so hard the door-step that the poor dog was flattened out like a pancake, and could not move a bit.

When the King came back he said:

"Hullo! some kind friend has brought me a new door-mat as a present," and he leaned down and stroked the soft hair with much pleasure. Then he wiped his feet on the new mat and went into the palace to tell the Queen.

When her Majesty saw the nice, soft door-mat she declared it was too good to be left outside; so she brought it into the parlor and put it on the floor before the fire-place.

The good King was sorry he had treated the dog so harshly, and for fear he might do some other dreadful thing he went back to the place where he had lost his temper and searched until he found it again, when he put it carefully away in his pocket where it would stay.

Then he returned to the palace an entered the parlor; but as he passed the mat, his new boots were so clumsy, he stumbled against the edge and pushed the mat together into a roll.

Immediately the dog gave a bark, got upon its legs and said:

"Well, this is better! Now I can breathe again, but while I was so flat I could not draw a single breath."

The monarch and his Queen were much surprised to find that what they had taken for a mat was only the dog, that had fallen so flat on their door-step; but they could not forbear laughing at his queer appearance. For, as the King had kicked the mat on the edge, the dog was more than six feet long, and no bigger around than a lead-pencil; which brought its font legs so far from its rear legs that it could scarcely turn around in the room without getting tangled up.

"But it is better than being a door-mat," said the dog; and the King and Queen agreed with him in this.

Then the King went away to tell the people he had found the dog again, and when he left the palace he slammed the front door behind him. The dog had started to follow the King out, so when the front door slammed it hit the poor animal so sharp a blow on the nose that it pushed his body together again; and, lo and behold! there was the dog in his natural shape, just as he was before the King kicked him.

After this the dog and the King agreed very well; for the King

L. Frank Baum

was careful not to kick, since he had recovered his temper, and the dog took care not to say anything that would provoke the King to anger.

And one day the dog saved the Kingdom and all the Valley of Mo from destruction, as I shall tell you another time.

THE FOURTH SURPRISE

THE PECULIAR PAINS OF FRUITCAKE ISLAND

Prince Zingle, who was the eldest of all the princes of the Valley of Mo, at one time became much irritated because the King, his father, would not allow him to milk the cow with the golden horns. This cow was a great favorite with the King, because she gave as large a quantity of ice-cream at a milking as an ordinary cow does of milk, and in the warm days this was an agreeable luxury. The King liked to keep the cow with the golden horns for his own use and that of the Queen; so Prince Zingle thought he was being abused, having a great fondness for ice-cream himself.

To be sure, there was the great fountain of ice-cream soda-water playing constantly in the courtyard, which was free to every one; but the Prince longed for what he could not have.

Therefore, being filled with anger against his father, the King, he wandered away until he chanced to come near to the castle of the Purple Dragon.

When the wicked monster saw the Prince, it decided that here was a splendid opportunity to make mischief; so it said, politely:

"Good morning, King Zingle."

"I am not a king—I am only a prince," replied Zingle.

L. Frank Baum

"What! not a king?" exclaimed the Dragon, as if surprised; "that is too bad."

"I can never be a king while my father lives," continued the Prince, "and it is impossible for him to die. So what can I do?"

"Since you ask my advice, I will tell you," answered the naughty Dragon. "Down near Rootbeer River, where the peanut trees grow, is a very deep hole in the ground. You must get the King to go and look into this hole, and while he is leaning over the edge, push him in. Of course, he will not die, for that, as you say, is impossible; but no one will know where to find him. So, your father being out of the way, you will be king in his place."

"That is surely good advice," said the Prince, "and I will go and do it at once. Then the cow with the golden horns will be mine, and I shall become the Monarch of Mo."

The Prince turned to go back to the palace, and as soon as he was out of sight, the horrid Dragon laughed to think what a fool it had made of the boy.

When Zingle saw his father he called him aside and said:

"Your Majesty, I have discovered something very funny at the bottom of the hole near the peanut trees. Come and see what it is."

So the King went with the Prince, without suspecting his evil design, and while he leaned over the hole the Prince gave him a sudden push. The next moment down fell the Monarch of Mo—way to the bottom!

Then Prince Zingle went back to the palace and began to milk the cow with the golden horns.

Now when the King found himself at the bottom of the hole he at first did not know what to do; so he sat down and thought about it. Presently a happy idea came into his head. He knew if only he was at the other end of the hole, he would be at the top instead of the bottom, and could make his escape. So the King took hold of the hole, and exerting all his strength, turned the hole upside down. Being now at the top he stepped upon the ground and walked back to the palace, where he caught Prince Zingle milking the cow with the golden horns.

"Oh, ho!" he said, "you wish to be King, do you? Well, we'll see about that!" Then he took the naughty Prince by the ear and led him into the palace, where he locked him up in a room from which he could not escape.

The King now sat himself down in an easy chair and began to think on how he could best punish the Prince, but after an hour of deep thought he was unable to decide on anything that seemed a sufficient chastisement for so great an offense.

At last he resolved to consult the Wise Donkey.

The Wise Donkey lived in a pretty little house away at the end of the Valley, for he didn't like to mix with the gay life at the court. He had not always been wise, but at one time was a very stupid donkey indeed, and he acquired his wisdom in this way.

One Friday afternoon, just as school was letting out, the stupid donkey strayed into the school-house, and the teachers and scholars were all so anxious to get home that they never noticed the donkey, but locked him up in the school-house and went away without knowing he was there.

No one came into the building from Friday afternoon until Monday morning; so the donkey got very hungry, and certainly would have starved had he not chanced to taste of a geography that was sticking out from one of the desks. The hungry donkey decided it was not so very bad, so he ate it all up. Then he ate an arithmetic, an algebra, and two first readers. After that he lay down and went to sleep; but becoming hungry again he awoke and commenced on the school library, which he completely devoured. This library comprised all the solid and substantial wisdom in the Valley of Mo, and when the janitor opened the school-house door on Monday morning, all the books of learning in the whole land had been eaten up by the stupid donkey.

You can readily understand that after he had digested all this knowledge he became very wise, and thereafter the King and the people often consulted the Wise Donkey when their own intelligence was at fault.

So now the monarch went to the donkey's house and told him of the Prince's wickedness, asking how he could best punish him.

The Wise Donkey thought about the matter for a moment and then replied:

"I do not know a worse punishment than a pain in the stomach. Among the books I ate in the school-house was a trigonometry, and before I had digested it I suffered very severe pains indeed."

"But I can not feed the Prince a trigonometry," returned the King. "You ate the last one yourself."

"True," answered the donkey; "but there are other things that cause pain in the stomach. You know there is a certain island in Rootbeer River that is made of fruit cake of a very rich quality. I advise you to put the Prince on this island and allow him nothing to eat except the fruit cake. Presently he will have violent pains in his stomach and will be punished as greatly as you could desire."

The King was well pleased with this plan, and having thanked the donkey for his wise advice hurried back to the palace.

Prince Zingle was now brought from his room and rowed in a

boat to the Fruit Cake Island in Rootbeer River, where he was left without any way to escape. He knew how to swim, to be sure, but it was forbidden by lawto swim in the Rootbeer, as many people came to this river to drink.

"You shall stay here," said the King, sternly, "until you are sorry for your wickedness; and you shall have nothing to eat but fruit cake."

The Prince laughed, because he thought the punishment was no punishment at all. When the King had rowed away in the boat and Zingle was left alone, he said to himself:

"Why, this is delightful! I shall have a jolly time here, and can eat all the cake I want, without any one scolding me for being greedy."

He broke off a large piece of the island where the raisins and citron were thickest, and commenced to eat it. But after a time he became tired of eating nothing but fruit cake, and longed for something to go with it. But the island did not contain a single thing except the cake of which it was composed.

Presently Prince Zingle began to have a pain inside him. He paid no attention to it at first, thinking it would pass away; but instead it grew more severe, so that he began to cry out; but no one heard him.

The pain steadily increased, and the Prince wept and rolled on the ground and began to feel exceeding sorry he had been so wicked. Finally he seized the telephone, which was connected with the palace, and called up the King.

"Hullo!" said the King's voice, in reply; "what's wanted?"

"I have a terrible pain," said the Prince, with a groan, "and I'm very sorry indeed that I pushed your Majesty down the hole. If you'll only take me off this dreadful island I'll be the best prince in all the Valley from this time forth!"

So the King sent the boat and had the Prince brought back to the palace, where he forgave his naughty actions. Being a kind parent he next fed his suffering son a blossom from a medicine tree, which quickly relieved his pain and led him to appreciate the pleasure of repentance.

THE FIFTH SURPRISE

THE MONARCH CELEBRATES HIS BIRTHDAY

There were great festivities in the Valley of Mo when the King had a birthday. The jolly monarch was born so many years ago that so every one had forgotten the date. One of the Wise Men said the King was born in February; another declared it was in May, and a third figured the great event happened in October. So the King issued a royal decree that he should have three birthdays every year, in order to be on the safe side; and whenever he happened to think of it he put in an odd birthday or two for luck. The King's birthdays came to be regarded as very joyful events, for on these occasions festivities of unusual magnificence were held, and everybody in the kingdom was invited to participate.

On one occasion the King, suddenly recollecting he had not celebrated his birthday for several weeks, announced a royal festival on a most elaborate scale. The cream-puff crop was an unusually large one, and the bushes were hanging full of the delicious ripe puffs, which were highly prized by the people of Mo.

So all the maidens got out their best dresses and brightest ribbons, and the young men carefully brushed their hair and polished their boots, and soon the streets leading to the palace were thronged with gay merry-makers.

When the guests were all assembled a grand feast was served, in which the newly-picked cream puffs were an important item.

Then the King stood up at the head of the table and ordered his ruby casket to be brought him, and when the people heard this they at once became quiet and attentive, for the Ruby Casket was one of the most curious things in the Valley. It was given the King many years before by the sorceress, Maetta, and whenever it was opened something was found in it that no living person had seen before.

So the people, and even the King himself, always watched the opening of the Ruby Casket with much curiosity, for they never knew what would be disclosed.

The King placed the casket on a small table before him, and then, after a solemn look at the expectant faces, he said, slowly:

"Giggle-gaggle-goo!" which was the magic word that opened the box.

At once the lid flew back, and the King peered within and exclaimed: "Ha!"

This made the guests more excited than before, for they did not know what he was saying "ha!" about; and they held their breaths when the King put his thumb and finger into the box and drew out a little wooden man about as big as my finger. He wore a blue jacket and a red cap and held a little brass horn in his hand.

The King stood the wooden man upon the table and then reached within the box and brought out another wooden man, dressed just the same as the other, and also holding a horn in his hand. This the King stood beside the first wooden man, and then took out another, and another, until ten little wooden men were standing in a row on the table, holding drums, and cymbals, and horns in their small, stiff hands.

"I declare," said the King, when he had stood them all up, "it's a little German band. But what a shame it is they can not play."

No sooner had the King uttered the word "play" than every little wooden man put his horn to his mouth, or beat his drum, or clashed his cymbal; and immediately they began to play such delicious music that all the people were delighted, and even the King clapped his hands in applause.

Just then from out the casket leaped a tiny Baby Elephant, about as large as a mouse, and began capering about on its toes. It was dressed in short, fluffy skirts, like those worn by a ballet-dancer, and it danced so funnily that all who saw it roared with laughter.

When the elephant stopped to rest, two pretty Green Frogs sprang from the casket and began to play leapfrog before the astonished guests, who had never before seen such a thing as a frog. The little green strangers jumped over each other quick as a flash, and finally one of them jumped down the other's throat. Then, as the Baby Elephant opened his mouth to yawn, the remaining frog jumped down the elephant's throat.

The audience was so much amused at this feat that the Baby Elephant thought he would see what he could do to please them; so he stood on his head and gave a great jump, and disappeared down his own throat, leaving the musicians to play by themselves.

Then all the young men caught the girls about their waists and began spinning around in a pretty dance of their own, and the fun continued until they were tired out.

The King thanked the tiny wooden musicians and put them back in the Ruby Casket. He did not offer to take up a collection for them, there being no money of any kind in the Valley of Mo. The casket was then carried back to the royal treasury, where it was guarded with much care when not in use.

Just then a young man approached the King, asking permission for the people to skate on the Crystal Lake, and his Majesty graciously consented.

As it was never cold in the Kingdom of Mo there was, of course, no ice for skating. But the Crystal Lake was composed of sugar-syrup, and the sun had candied the surface of the lake, so it had become solid enough to skate on, and was, moreover, as smooth as glass.

It was not often the King allowed skating there, for he feared some one might break through the crust; but as it was his birthday he could refuse the people nothing. So presently hundreds of the boys and girls were skating swiftly on the Crystal Lake and having rare sport; for it was just as good as ice, without being cold or damp.

In the center there was one place where the crust was quite thin, and just as the merriment was at its height, crack! went the ice—or candy, rather—and down into the sugar-syrup sank the Princess Truella, and the Prince Jollikin, and the King's royal chamberlain, Nuphsed.

Down and down they went until they reached the bottom of the lake; and there they stood, stuck fast in the syrup and unable to move a bit, while all the people gathered on the shore to look at them, the lake being as clear as the clearest water.

Of course, this calamity put an end to further skating, and the King rushed around asking every one how he could get his daughter and his son and his royal chamberlain out of the mass. But no one could tell him.

Finally the King consulted the Wise Donkey; and after he had thought the matter over and consulted his learning, the donkey advised his Majesty to fish for them.

"Fish!" exclaimed the King; "how can we do that?"

"Take a fish-line and put a sinker on it, to make it sink through the syrup. Then bait the end of the line with the thing that each one of them likes best. In that way you can catch hold of them and draw them out of the lake."

"Well," said the King, "I'll try it, for of course you know what you are talking about."

"Have you ever eaten a geography?" demanded the Wise Donkey.

"No," said the King.

"Well, I have," declared the donkey, haughtily; "and what I don't know about lakes and such things isn't in the geography."

So the King went back to the Crystal Lake and got a strong fish-line, which he tied to the end of a long pole. Then he put a sinker on the end of the line and was ready for the bait.

"What does the Princess Truella like best?" he asked the Queen.

"I'm sure I do not know," replied the royal lady; "but you might try her with a kiss."

So one of the nicest young men sent a kiss to the Princess, and the King tied it to the end of the line and put it in the lake. The sinker carried it down through the sugar-syrup until the kiss was just before the sweet, red lips of the pretty Princess. She took the kiss at once, as the Queen had guessed, and the King pulled up the line, with the Princess at the end of it, until he finally landed her on the shore.

Then all the people shouted for joy and the Queen took the Princess Truella home to change her clothes, for they were very sticky.

L. Frank Baum

"What does the Prince Jollikin like best?" asked the King.

"A laugh!" replied a dozen at once, for every one knew the Prince's failing.

Then one of the girls laughed quite hard, and the King tied it to the end of the line and dropped it into the lake. The Prince caught the laugh at once, and was quickly drawn from the syrup and likewise sent home to change his clothes.

Then the King looked around on the people and asked:

"What does the Chamberlain Nuphsed like best?"

But they were all silent, for Nuphsed liked so many things it was difficult to say which he liked best. So again the King was obliged to go to the Wise Donkey, in order to find out how he should bait the line to catch the royal chamberlain.

The Wise Donkey happened to be busy that day over his own affairs and was annoyed at being consulted so frequently without receiving anything in return for his wisdom. But he pretended to consider the matter, as was his wont, and said:

"I believe the royal chamberlain is fond of apples. Try to catch him with a red apple."

At this the King and his people hunted all over the kingdom, and at last found a tree with one solitary red apple growing on a little branch nearly at the top. But unfortunately some one had sawed off the trunk of the tree, close up to the branches, and had carried it away and chopped it up for kindling wood. For this reason there was no way to climb the tree to secure the apple.

While the King and the people were considering how they might get into the tree, Prince Thinkabit came up to them and asked what they wanted.

"We want the apple," replied the King, "but some one has cut away the tree trunk, so that we can not climb up."

Prince Thinkabit rubbed the top of his head a minute, to get his brain into good working order. It was a habit he had acquired. Then he walked to the bank of the river, which was near, and whistled three times. Immediately a school of fishes swam up to him, and one of the biggest cried out:

"Good afternoon, Prince Thinkabit; what can we do for you?"

"I wish to borrow a flying fish for a few minutes," replied the Prince.

Scarcely had he spoken when a fish flew out of the river and perched upon his shoulder. Then he walked up to the tree and said to the fish: "Get me the apple."

The flying fish at once flew into the tree and bit off the stem of the apple, which fell down and hit the King on the nose, for, unfortunately, he was standing exactly under it. Then the Prince thanked the flying fish and sent it back to the river, and the King, having first put a plaster over his nose, took the apple and started for the Crystal Lake, followed by all his people.

But when the apple was fastened to the fish-line and let down through the syrup to the royal chamberlain, Nuphsed refused to touch it.

"He doesn't like it," said the King, with a sigh; and he went again to the Wise Donkey.

"Didn't he want the apple?" asked the donkey, as if surprised. But you must know he was not surprised at all, as he had planned to get the apple for himself.

"No, indeed," replied the King. "We had an awful job to find the apple, too."

"Where is it?" inquired the donkey.

"Here," said the King, taking it out of his pocket.

The donkey took the apple, looked at it thoughtfully for a moment, and then ate it up and smacked his lips, for he was especially fond of red apples.

"What shall we do now?" asked the King.

"I believe the thing Nuphsed likes best is a kind word. Bait the line with that, and you may catch him."

So the King went again to the lake, and having put a kind word on the fish-line quickly succeeded in bringing the royal chamberlain to the shore in safety. You can well imagine poor Nuphsed was glad enough to be on dry land after his long immersion in the sugar-syrup.

And now that all had been rescued from the Crystal Lake, the King put a rope around the broken crust and stuck up a sign that said "Danger!" so that no one else would fall in.

After that the festivities began again, and as there were no further accidents the King's birthday ended very happily.

THE SIXTH SURPRISE

KING SCOWLEYOW AND HIS CAST-IRON MAN

Across the mountains at the north of the Valley of Mo there reigned a wicked King named Scowleyow, whose people lived in caves and mines and dug iron and tin out of the rocks and melted them into bars. These bars they then carried away and sold for money.

King Scowleyow hated the Monarch of Mo and all his people, because they lived so happily and cared nothing for money; and he would have sent his army into the Valley to destroy the merry people who dwelt there had he not been afraid of the sharp swords that grew on their trees, which they knew so well how to use against their foes.

So King Scowleyow pondered for a long time how to destroy the Valley of Mo without getting hurt himself; and at last he hit on a plan he believed would succeed.

He put all his mechanics to work and built a great man out of cast-iron, with machinery inside of him. When he was wound up the Cast-iron Man could roar, and roll his eyes, and gnash his teeth and march across the Valley, crushing trees and houses to the earth as he went. For the Cast-iron Man was as tall as a church and as heavy as iron could make him, and each of his feet was as big as a barn.

It took a long time to build this man, as you may suppose; but

L. Frank Baum

King Scowleyow was so determined to ruin the pretty Valley of Mo that he made his men work night and day, and at last the Cast-iron Man was ready to be wound up and sent on his journey of destruction.

They stood him on the top of the mountain, with his face toward the Beautiful Valley, and began to wind him up. It took a hundred men a whole week to do this; but at last he was tightly wound, and the wicked King Scowleyow stood ready to touch the spring that made him go.

"One—two—three!" said the King, and touched the spring with his ringer.

The Cast-iron Man gave so terrible a roar that he even frightened the men who had made him; and then he rolled his eyes till they flashed fire, and gnashed his teeth till the noise sounded like thunder.

The next minute he raised one great foot and stepped forward, crushing fifty trees that stood in his path, and then away he went, striding down the mountain, destroying everything that stood in his way, and nearing with every step the Beautiful Valley of Mo.

The King and his people were having a game of ball that day, and the dog was acting as umpire. Suddenly, just as Prince Jollikin had made a home run and everybody was applauding him, a terrible roaring noise sounded in their ears, and they heard a great crashing of trees on the mountain side and saw a monstrous man approaching the Valley.

The people were so frightened they stood perfectly still, being unable to move through surprise and terror; but the dog ran with all his might toward the mountain to see what was the matter. Just as the dog reached the foot of the mountain the Cast-iron Man came tramping along and stepped into the Valley, where he ruined in one instant a large bed of lady-fingers and a whole patch of ripe pumpkin pies. Indeed, the entire Valley would soon have been destroyed had not the Cast-iron Man stubbed his toe against the dog and fallen flat on his face, where he lay roaring and gnashing his teeth, but unable to do any further harm.

Presently the King and his people recovered from their fright and gathered around their prostrate foe, marveling at his great size and strength.

"Had you not tripped him up," said the King to the dog, "this giant would certainly have destroyed my kingdom. Who do you suppose was so wicked as to send this monster to crush us?"

"It must have been King Scowleyow," declared the dog, "for no one else would care to harm you, and the giant came from the direction of the wicked King's country."

"Yes," replied the monarch, thoughtfully, "it must indeed have been Scowleyow; and it was a very unkind act, for we never harmed him in any way. But what shall we do with this great man? If he is left here he will scare all the children with his roarings, and none of the ladies will care to walk near this end of the Valley. He is so heavy that not all of us together could lift him, and even if we succeeded we have no place to put him where he would be out of the way."

This was indeed true; so all the people sat down in a circle around the Cast-iron Man and thought upon the matter intently for the space of an hour.

Then the monarch asked, solemnly, as became the importance of the occasion:

"Has any one thought of a way to get rid of him?"

The people shook their heads gravely and thought deeply for another hour. At the end of that time the dog suddenly laughed, and called out in a voice so loud that it startled them:

L. Frank Baum

"I have thought of a way!"

"Good!" exclaimed the King. "Let us hear your plan."

"You see," explained the dog, "the Cast-iron Man is now lying on his face. If we could only roll him over on to his back, and then raise him to his feet again, he would be turned around, and would march straight back to where he came from, and do us no further harm."

"That is a capital idea," replied the King. "But how can we roll him over, or make him stand up?"

That puzzled them all for a while, but by and by Prince Thinkabit, who was a very clever young man, announced his readiness to undertake the job.

"First, bring me a feather," commanded the Prince.

The royal chamberlain hunted around and soon found for him a long, fluffy feather. Taking this in his hand the Prince approached the Cast-iron Man and tickled him under the left arm with the end of the feather.

"Ouch!" said the Cast-iron Man, giving a jump and rolling completely over, so that he lay on his back.

"Hurrah!" cried the people, clapping their hands with joy at this successful stratagem; "the Prince is a very wise Prince, indeed!"

Prince Thinkabit took off his hat and bowed politely to them in return for the compliment. Then he said:

"Bring me a pin."

So Nuphsed brought him a pin with a very sharp point, and the Prince took it and walked up to the Cast-iron Man, and gave him a sharp prod in the back with the point of the pin.

"Ouch!" again yelled the Cast-iron Man, giving at the same time such a great jump that he leaped square on his feet. But now, to their joy, they saw he was facing the mountains instead of the Valley.

As soon as the Cast-iron Man stood up the machinery began to work again, and he marched with great steps up the mountain side and over into the kingdom of the wicked Scowleyow, where he crushed the King and all his people, and laid waste the land wherever he went.

And that was their punishment for being envious of the good people of Mo.

As to the fate of the Cast-iron Man, he was wound up so tightly that he kept walking straight on until he reached the sea, where he stepped into the water, went down to the bottom, and stuck fast in the mud.

And I have no doubt he is there to this day.

L. Frank Baum

THE SEVENTH SURPRISE

TIMTOM AND THE PRINCESS PATTYCAKE

Now of all the monarch's daughters the most beautiful by far was the Princess Pattycake. The deep blue of her eyes made even the sky envious, and the moss roses blushed when they saw the delicate bloom on her cheeks. The long strands of her silken hair were brighter than sunbeams, while her ears were like two tiny pink shells from the seashore. Indeed, there was nothing in all the Valley so dainty and pretty as Princess Pattycake, and many young men would have loved her had they dared. But, alas! the Princess had a most terrible temper, and never was pleased with anything; so the young men, and even the old ones, were afraid to come near her.

She scolded from morning till night; she stamped her pretty foot with rage when any one spoke to her; and if ever her brothers tried to reason with her she boxed their ears so soundly that they were glad to let her alone. Even the good Queen could not love Pattycake as she did her other children, and the King often sighed when he thought of the ugly disposition of his beautiful daughter. Of course no one cared very much for her society, and she sat in her room all day long, refusing to join the others in their sports and games, and becoming more moody and bad-tempered the older she grew.

One day a young man came to the court to bring pickled peaches to his Majesty, the King. The youth's name was Timtom, and he lived so far away and came so seldom to court that never before had he seen the Princess Pattycake.

When he looked into her sweet, blue eyes he loved her at once for her beauty, and being both brave and bold he went directly to the King and asked for Pattycake's hand in marriage.

His Majesty was naturally surprised at so strange a request; so he said to the young man:

"What does the Princess say? Does she love you?"

"I do not know," replied Timtom, "for I have never spoken with her."

"Well," said the King, much amazed at the ignorance and temerity of the youth, "go and speak to my daughter about the matter, and then come and tell me what she replies."

Timtom went at once to the room where Princess Pattycake was moodily sitting, and said, boldly:

"I should like to marry you."

"What!" screamed the Princess, in a great rage; "marry me! Go away this instant, you impudent boy, or I shall throw my shoe at your head!"

Timtom was both surprised and shocked at this outburst, but he realized that the Princess had a remarkably bad temper. Still he was not moved from his purpose, for she was so pretty he decided not to abandon the attempt to win her.

"Do not be angry, for I love you," he pleaded, looking bravely into Pattycake's blue eyes.

"Love me?" echoed the surprised Princess; "that is not possible! Every one else hates me."

"They do not hate you," ventured Timtom; "it is your temper

L. Frank Baum

they hate."

"But my temper and I are one," answered the Princess, harshly, as she stamped her foot.

"Surely that is not so," returned the young man, "for certainly I love you, while your temper I do not like a bit. Don't you think you could love me?"

"Perhaps I might, if you could cure my bad temper; but my temper will not allow me to love any one. In fact, I believe that unless you go away at once I shall be obliged to box your ears!"

There seemed to be no help for her, so Timtom left the room sadly, and going to the King, told him what she had said.

"Then that is the end of the matter," declared the King, "for no one can cure Pattycake of her bad temper."

"I am resolved to try, nevertheless," replied Timtom, "and, if I succeed, you must give me the Princess in marriage."

"I will, and my blessing into the bargain," answered the King, heartily.

Then Timtom left the court, and went back to his father's house, where he thought on the problem for a week and a day. At the end of that time he was no nearer solving it than he was before; but his mother, who had noticed that her boy was in trouble, now came to him to ask the cause of his sad looks. Timtom told her all about the Princess Pattycake, and of his love for her, and the evil temper that would not be cured.

His mother gave him her sympathy, and after some thought, said to him: "You must go to the sorceress Maetta and ask her assistance. She is a good lady, and a friend to all the King's family. I am quite sure she will aid you, if only you can find your way to the castle in which she lives."

"Where is this castle?" asked Timtom, brightening up.

"Away to the south, in the midst of a thick wood," answered his mother.

"Then," said he, sturdily, "if this castle exists, I will surely find it, for to win Pattycake is my only hope of happiness."

The next day he set out on his journey, filled with the hope of finding Maetta's castle and securing her assistance.

Before he had gone very far a snow-storm began to rage. Now, the snow-storms in Mo are different from ours, for the snow is popcorn, and on this day it fell so thick and fast that poor Timtom had much difficulty in wading through it. He was obliged to stop frequently to rest, and ate a great deal of the popcorn that cumbered his path, for it was nicely buttered and salted.

Finally, to his joy, it stopped snowing, and then he was able to walk along easily until he came to the River of Needles.

When he looked on this river he was nearly discouraged, and could not think of a way to get across; for instead of water the river flowed a perfect stream of sharp, glittering needles.

Sitting down on the bank, he was wondering what he should do when to his astonishment a small but sharp and disagreeable voice said to him:

"Where are you going, stranger?"

Timtom looked down between his feet and saw a black spider, which sat on a blade of grass and watched him curiously.

"I am on my way to visit the sorceress Maetta," replied Timtom; "But I can not get across the River of Needles."

"They are very sharp, and would make a thousand holes

L. Frank Baum

through you in an instant," remarked the spider, thoughtfully. "But perhaps I can help you. If you are willing to grant me a favor in return, I will gladly build a bridge, so you may cross the river in safety."

"What is the favor?" he asked.

"I have lost an eye, and you must ask the sorceress to give me a new one, for I can see but half as well as I could before."

"I will gladly do this for you," said Timtom.

"Very well; then I will build you a bridge," promised the spider; "but if you have not the eye with you when you return I shall destroy the bridge, and you will never be able to get home again."

The young man agreed to this, for he was anxious to proceed. So the spider threw a web across the river, and then another, and another, until it had made a bridge of spider-web strong enough for Timtom to cross over.

It bent and swayed when his weight was on the slender bridge, but it did not break, and after he was safe across he thanked the spider and renewed his promise to bring back the eye. Then he hurried away on his journey, for he had lost much time at the river.

But, to his dismay, the young man shortly came to a deep gulf, that barred his way as completely as had the River of Needles. He peered down into it and saw it had no bottom, but opened away off at the other side of the world. Here was an obstacle which might well dishearten the boldest traveler, and Timtom was so grieved that he sat down on the brink and wept tears of disappointment.

"What is troubling you?" asked a soft voice in his ear.

Turning his head the youth saw a beautiful white bird sitting beside him.

"I wish to visit the castle of the sorceress Maetta on very important business," he replied, "but I can not get over the gulf."

"I could carry you over with ease," said the bird, "and shall gladly do so if, in return, you promise to grant me one favor."

"What is the favor?" inquired Timtom.

"I have forgotten my song, through having a sore throat for a long time," replied the bird. "So, try as I may, I can not sing a single note. If you will agree to bring me a new song from the sorceress I will take you over the gulf, and bring you back when you return. But unless you bring the song I shall not carry you over again."

Timtom joyfully agreed to this bargain, and then, sitting on the bird's neck, he was borne safely across the deep gulf.

After continuing his journey for an hour without further interruption he saw before him the edge of a great wood, and knew that in the midst of this forest of trees was the castle of Maetta.

He thought then that his difficulties were all over, and tramped bravely on until he reached the wood. What, now, was the youth's horror on discovering on one side of his path a great lion, crouched ready to spring on any one who ventured to enter the wood, while on the other side was a monstrous tiger, likewise prepared to attack any intruder. The fierce beasts were growling terribly, and their eyes glowed like balls of fire.

Timtom gladly would have turned back had such a thing been possible, for his heart was full of fear. But he remembered that without the bird's song and the spider's eye he could never reach home again. He also thought of the pretty face of

L. Frank Baum

Princess Pattycake, and this gave him courage. Resolving to perish, if need be, rather than fail in his adventure, the youth stepped boldly forward, and when he approached the snarling guardians of the forest he gave one bound and dashed into the wood.

At the same moment the lion leaped at him from one side and the tiger from the other, and no doubt they would have devoured him had not Timtom's foot slipped just then and thrown him flat on the ground. The lion and the tiger therefore met in mid air, and each one thinking it had hold of Timtom, tried to tear him to pieces, with the result that in a few moments they had devoured each other instead of him.

The youth now strode rapidly through the wood, and was getting along famously when he came to a high wall of jasper that completely blocked his way. It was smooth as glass, and Timtom saw no way of climbing over it.

While he stood wondering how he might overcome this new obstacle a gray rabbit hopped out from the bushes and asked:

"Where do you wish to go, stranger?"

"To the castle of the sorceress Maetta," answered Timtom.

"Well, perhaps I can assist you," said the rabbit. "I need a new tail badly, for my old one is merely a stump, and no use at all in fly-time. If you will be kind enough to get me a new tail from the sorceress Maetta—a long, nice, bushy tail—I will dig under the wall, and so make a passage for you to the other side."

"I shall be pleased to return the favor by bringing you the tail," declared Timtom, eagerly.

"Very well; then you shall see how fast I can work," returned the rabbit. Immediately it began digging away with its little paws, and in a very short time had made a hole large enough for Timtom to crawl under the wall.

"If you do not bring the tail," said the rabbit, in a warning voice, "I shall fill up the hole again, so that you will be unable to get back."

"Oh, I shall bring the tail, never fear," answered the youth, and hurried away toward the castle of Maetta, which was now visible through the trees.

The castle was built of pure, white marble, and was very big and beautiful. It stood in a lovely garden filled with blue roses and pink buttercups, where fountains of gold spouted showers of diamonds, and rubies, and emeralds, and amethysts, all of which sparkled in the sun so gorgeously that it made Timtom's eyes ache just to look at them.

However, he had not come to admire these things, gorgeous and beautiful though they were, but to win the Princess Pattycake; so he walked to the entrance of the castle, and seeing no one about, entered the great door-way and passed through.

He found himself in a passage-way covered with mother-of-pearl, where many electric lights were hidden in shells of most exquisite tintings. At the other end of the passage was a door studded with costly gems.

Timtom walked up to this door and knocked on it. Immediately it swung open, and the youth found himself in a chamber entirely covered with diamonds. In the center was a large diamond throne, and on this sat Maetta, clothed in a pure white gown, with a crown of diamonds on her brow and in her hand a golden scepter tipped with one enormous diamond that glowed like a ball of fire. Above the throne was a diamond-covered chandelier, with hundreds of electric lights, and these made the Grand Chamber of Diamonds glitter so brightly that Timtom was nearly blinded, and had to shade his eyes with his hand.

L. Frank Baum

But after a few moments he grew accustomed to the brightness and advancing to the throne fell on his knees before the sorceress and begged her earnestly to grant him her assistance.

Maetta was the most beautiful woman in all the world, but she was likewise gracious and kind. So she smiled sweetly on the youth, bidding him, in a voice like a silver bell, to arise from his knees and sit before her. Timtom obeyed and looked around for a chair, but could see none in the room. The lady made a motion with her scepter and instantly at his side appeared a splendid diamond chair, in which the young man seated himself, finding it remarkably comfortable.

"Tell me what you desire," said the sorceress, in her sweet voice.

"I love the Princess Pattycake," replied Timtom, without hesitation. "But she has so evil a disposition that she has refused to marry me unless I am able to cure her of her bad temper, which not only makes her miserable but ruins the pleasure of every one about her. So, knowing your power and the kindness of your heart, I have been bold enough to seek your castle, that I might crave your assistance, without which I can not hope to accomplish my purpose."

Maetta waved her scepter thrice above her head, and a golden pill dropped at Timtom's feet.

"Your request is granted," she said. "If you can induce the Princess to swallow this pill her evil temper will disappear, and I know she will love you dearly for having cured her. Take great care of it, for if it should be lost I can not give you another. Do you wish me to grant any other request before you return to the court?"

Then Timtom remembered the rabbit, and the bird, and the spider, and told Maetta how he had promised to bring back a gift for each of them.

So the kind sorceress gave him a nice, bushy tail for the rabbit, and a very pretty song for the bird, and a new, bright eye for the spider. These Timtom put in a little red box and placed the box carefully in his pocket. But the golden pill he tied into the corner of his handkerchief, for that was more precious than the rest.

Having thanked the generous lady for her kindness and respectfully kissed the white hand she held out to him, Timtom left the Chamber of Diamonds and was soon proceeding joyfully on his homeward way.

In a short time he reached the wall of jasper, but the rabbit was not to be seen. So, while he awaited its coming, he lay down to rest, and being tired by the long journey was soon fast asleep. And while he slept a Sly Fox stole out from the wood and discovered Timtom lying on the ground.

"Oh, ho!" said the Sly Fox to himself, "this young man has been to visit the sorceress, and I'll warrant he has some fine gift from her in that little red box I see sticking out from his pocket. I must try to steal that box and see what is in it!"

Then, while the youth slumbered, unconscious of danger, the Sly Fox carefully drew the little red box from his pocket, and, taking it in his mouth, ran off into the woods with it.

Soon after this the rabbit came back, and when it saw Timtom lying asleep it awakened him and asked:

"Where is my new tail?"

"Oh, I have brought you a fine one," replied Timtom, with a smile. "It is in this little red box." But when he searched for the box he discovered it had been stolen.

So great was his distress at the loss that the gray rabbit was sorry for him.

L. Frank Baum

"I shall never be able to get home again," he moaned, weeping tears of despair, "for all the gifts Maetta gave me are now lost forever!"

"Never mind," said the rabbit, "I shall allow you to go under the wall without giving me the tail, for I know you tried to keep your promise. I suppose I can make this stubby tail do a while longer, since it is the only one I ever possessed. But beware when you come to the bird and the spider, for they will not be so kind to you as I am. The bird has no heart at all, and the spider's heart is hard as a stone. Still I advise you to keep up your courage, for if you are brave and fearless you may succeed in getting home, after all. If you can not cross the gulf and the River of Needles, you are welcome to come back and live with me."

Hearing this, Timtom dried his eyes and thanked the kind rabbit, after which he crawled under the wall and resumed his journey. He became more cheerful as he trudged along, for the golden pill was still safe in the corner of his handkerchief.

When he came to the white bird and began to explain how it was he had lost the song and could not keep his promise, the bird became very angry and refused to listen to his excuses. Nor could he induce it to carry him again across the gulf.

"I shall keep my word," declared the bird, stiffly; "for I warned you that if you returned without the song I should refuse to assist you further."

Poor Timtom was at his wits' end to know what to do; so he sat down near the brink of the gulf and twirled his thumbs and tried to keep up his courage and think of some plan, while the white bird strutted around in a cold and stately manner.

Now it seems that just about this time the Sly Fox reached his den and opened the little red box to see what was in it. The spider's eye, being small, rolled out into the moss and was lost. The fox thought he would put the bushy tail on himself and see if it would not add to his beauty, and while he did this the song escaped from the box and was blown by the wind directly to the spot where Timtom was sitting beside the gulf.

He happened to hear the song coming, so he took off his hat and caught it, after which he called to the bird that he had found the song again.

"Then I shall keep my promise," said the bird. "First, however, let me try the song and see if it is suited to my voice."

So he tried the song and liked it fairly well.

"It sounds something like a comic opera," said the bird, "but, after all, it will serve my purpose very nicely."

A minute later Timtom rejoiced to find himself on the other side of the gulf, and so much nearer home. But when he came to the River of Needles there was more trouble in store for him, for the spider became so angry at the loss of its eye that it tore down the spider-web bridge, and refused to build another.

This was indeed discouraging to the traveler, and he sat down beside the river and looked longingly at the farther shore. The spider paid no attention to him, but curled up and went to sleep, and the needles looked at him curiously out of their small eyes as they flowed by in an endless stream.

After a time a wren came flying along, and when it noticed the look of despair on Timtom's face the little creature perched on his shoulder and asked:

"What is your trouble, young man?"

Timtom related his adventures to the sympathetic wren, and when he came to the loss of the spider's eye and the refusal of the spiteful creature to allow him to cross the bridge, the wren exclaimed, with every appearance of surprise:

L. Frank Baum

"A spider's eye, did you say? Why, I believe that is what I have here in my claw!"

"Where?" cried Timtom, eagerly.

The wren hopped into his lap, and carefully opening one of its tiny claws disclosed the identical spider's eye which Maetta had given him.

"That is wonderful!" exclaimed Timtom, in amazement. "But where did you get it?"

"I found it in the wood, hidden in the moss near the den of the Sly Fox. It is so bright and sparkling I thought I would take it home for my children to play with. But now, as you seem to want it so badly, I shall have much pleasure in restoring it to you."

Timtom thanked the little wren most gratefully, and called to the spider to come and get its eye. When the spider tried the eye, and found that it fitted perfectly and was even brighter than the old one, it became very polite to the young man, and soon built the bridge again.

Having passed over the glittering needles in safety Timtom pushed forward on his way, being urged to haste by the delays he had suffered. When he reached the place where he had encountered the snow-storm, he found the birds had eaten all the pop-corn, so he was able to proceed without interruption.

At last he reached the Monarch of Mo's palace and demanded an audience with the Princess Pattycake. But the young lady, being in an especially bad temper that day, positively refused to see him.

Having overcome so many obstacles, Timtom did not intend to be thwarted by a sulky girl, so he walked boldly to the room where the Princess sat alone, every one being afraid to go near her.

"Good day, my dear Pattycake," he said pleasantly; "I have come to cure your bad temper."

"I do not want to be cured!" cried the Princess, angrily. "Go away at once, or I shall hurt you!"

"I shall not go away until you have promised to marry me," replied Timtom, firmly.

At this Pattycake began to scream with rage, and threw her shoe straight at his head. Timtom dodged the shoe and paid no attention to the naughty action, but continued to look at the pretty Princess smilingly. Seeing this, Pattycake rushed forward and seizing him by his hair began to pull with all her strength. At the same time she opened her mouth to scream, and while it was open Timtom threw the golden pill down her throat.

Immediately the Princess released his hair and sank at his feet sobbing and trembling, while she covered her pretty face with her hands to hide her blushes and shame.

Timtom tenderly patted her bowed head, and tried to comfort her, saying:

"Do not weep, sweetheart; for the bad temper has left you at last, and now every one will love you dearly."

"Can you forgive me for having been so naughty?" asked Pattycake, looking up at him pleadingly from her sweet blue eyes.

"I have forgiven you already," answered Timtom, promptly; "for it was not you, but the temper, that made you so naughty."

The Princess Pattycake dried her tears and kissed Timtom, promising to marry him; and together they went to seek the King and Queen. Those good people were greatly delighted at

L. Frank Baum

the change in their daughter, and consented at once to the betrothal.

A week later there was a great feast in the Valley of Mo, and much rejoicing among the people, for it was the wedding-day of Timtom and the Princess Pattycake.

THE EIGHTH SURPRISE

THE BRAVERY OF PRINCE JOLLIKIN

There is no country so delightful but that it suffers some disadvantages, and so it was with the Valley of Mo. At times the good people were obliged to leave their games and sports to defend themselves against a foe or some threatened disaster. But there was one danger they never suspected, which at last came upon them very suddenly.

Away at the eastern end of the Valley was a rough plain, composed entirely of loaf sugar covered with boulders of rock candy which were piled up in great masses reaching nearly to the foot of the mountains, containing many caves and recesses.

The people seldom came here, as there was nothing to tempt them, the rock candy being very hard and difficult to walk on.

In one of the great hollows formed by the rock candy lived a monstrous Gigaboo, completely shut in by the walls of its cavern. It had been growing and growing for so many years that it had attained an enormous size.

For fear you may not know what a Gigaboo is I shall describe this one. Its body was round, like that of a turtle, and on its back was a thick shell. From the center of the body rose a long neck, much like that of a goose, with a most horrible looking head perched on the top of it. This head was round as a ball, and had four mouths on the sides of it and seven eyes set in a circle and projecting several inches from the head. The Gigaboo walked on ten short but thick legs, and in front of its body were two long arms, tipped with claws like those of a lobster. So sharp and strong were these claws that the creature could pinch a tree in two easily. Its eyes were remarkably bright and glittering, one being red in color, another green, and the others yellow, blue, black, purple and crimson.

It was a dreadful monster to see—only no one had yet seen it, for it had grown up in the confinement of its cave.

But one day the Gigaboo became so big and strong that in turning around it broke down the walls of the cavern, and finding itself at liberty, the monster walked out into the lovely Valley of Mo to see how much evil it could do.

The first thing the Gigaboo came to was a large orchard of preserved apricots, and after eating a great quantity of the preserves it wilfully cut off the trees with its sharp claws and utterly ruined them. Why the Gigaboo should have done this I can not tell; but scientists say these creatures are by nature destructive, and love to ruin everything they come across.

One of the people, being in the neighborhood, came on the monster and witnessed its terrible deeds; whereupon he ran in great terror to tell the King that the Gigaboo was on them and ready to destroy the entire valley. Although no one had ever before seen a Gigaboo, or even heard of one, the news was so serious that in a short time the King and many of his people came to the place where the monster was, all having hastily armed themselves with swords and spears.

But when they saw the Gigaboo they were afraid, and stood gazing at it in alarm, without knowing what to do or how to attack it.

"Who among us can hope to conquer this great beast?" asked the King, in dismay. "Yet something must be done, or soon we shall not have a tree left standing in all the Valley of Mo." The people looked at one another in a frightened way, but no one volunteered his services or offered to advise the monarch what to do.

At length Prince Jollikin, who had been watching the monster earnestly, stepped forward and offered to fight the Gigaboo alone.

"In a matter of this kind," said he, "one man is as good as a dozen. So you will all stand back while I see where the beast can best be attacked."

"Is your sword sharp?" asked his father, the King, anxiously.

"It was the sharpest on the tree," replied the Prince. "If I fail to kill the monster, at least it can not kill me, although it may cause me some annoyance. At any rate, our trees must be saved, so I will do the best I can."

With this manly speech he walked straight toward the Gigaboo, which, when it saw him approaching, raised and lowered its long neck and twirled its head around, so that all the seven eyes might get a glimpse of its enemy.

Now you must remember, when you read what follows, that no inhabitant of the Valley of Mo can ever be killed by anything. If one is cut to pieces, the pieces still live; and, although this seems strange, you will find, if you ever go to this queer Valley, that it is true. Perhaps it was the knowledge of this fact that made Prince Jollikin so courageous.

"If I can but manage to cut off that horrible head with my sword," thought he, "the beast will surely die."

So the Prince rushed forward and made a powerful stroke at its neck; but the blow fell short, and cut off, instead, one of the Gigaboo's ten legs. Quick as lightning the monster put out a claw and nipped the Prince's arm which held the sword, cutting it from its body. As the sword fell the Prince caught it in his other hand and struck again; but the blow fell on the beast's shell, and did no harm.

The Gigaboo, now very angry, at once nipped off the Prince's left arm with one of its claws, and his head with the other. The arm fell on the ground and the head rolled down a little hill behind some bonbon bushes. The Prince, having lost both arms, and his head as well, now abandoned the fight and turned to run, knowing it would be folly to resist the monster further. But the Gigaboo gave chase, and so swiftly did its nine legs carry it that soon it overtook the Prince and nipped off both his legs.

Then, its seven eyes flashing with anger, the Gigaboo turned toward the rest of the people, as if seeking a new enemy; but the brave Men of Mo, seeing the sad plight of their Prince and being afraid of the awful nippers on the beast's claws, decided to run away; which they did, uttering as they went loud cries of terror.

But had they looked back they might not have gone so fast nor so far; for when the Gigaboo heard their cries it, in turn, became frightened, having been accustomed all its life to silence; so that it rushed back to its cavern of rock candy and hid itself among the boulders.

When Prince Jollikin's head stopped rolling, he opened his eyes and looked about him, but could see no one; for the people and the Gigaboo had now gone. So, being unable to move, he decided to lie quiet for a time, and this was not a pleasant thing for an active young man like the Prince to do. To be sure, he could wiggle his ears a bit, and wink his eyes; but that was the extent of his powers. After a few minutes, because he had a cheerful disposition and wished to keep himself amused, he began to whistle a popular song; and then, becoming interested in the tune, he whistled it over again with variations.

The Prince's left leg, lying a short distance away, heard his whistle, and, recognizing the variations, at once ran up to the head.

"Well," said the Prince, "here is a part of me, at any rate. I wonder where the rest of me can be."

Just then, hearing the sound of his voice, the right leg ran up to the head. "Where is my body?" asked the Prince. But the legs did not know.

"Pick up my head and place it on top of my legs," continued the Prince; "then, with my eyes and your feet, we can hunt around until we find the rest of me."

Obeying this command, the legs took the head and started off; and perhaps you can imagine how funny the Prince's head looked perched on his legs, with neither body nor arms.

After a careful search they found the body lying upon the ground at the foot of a shrimp-salad tree. But nothing more could be done without the arms; so they next searched for those, and, having discovered them, the legs kicked them to where the body lay.

The arms now took the head from the legs and put the legs on the body where they belonged. Then the right arm stuck the left arm in its place, after which the left arm picked up the right arm and placed it also where it belonged. Then all that remained was for the Prince to place his head on his shoulders, and there he was—as good as new!

He picked up his sword, and was feeling himself all over to see if he was put together right, when he chanced to look up and saw the Gigaboo again coming toward him. The beast had recovered from its fright, and, tempted by its former success, again ventured forth.

But Prince Jollikin did not intend to be cut to pieces a second time. He quickly climbed a tree and hid himself among the branches.

Presently the Gigaboo came to the tree and reached its head up to eat a cranberry tart. Quick as a flash the Prince swung his sword downward, and so true was his stroke that he cut off the monster's head with ease.

Then the Gigaboo rolled over on its back and died, for wild and ferocious beasts may be killed in Mo as well as in other parts of the world. Having vanquished his enemy, Prince Jollikin climbed down from the tree and went to tell the people that the Gigaboo was dead.

When they heard this joyful news they gave their Prince three cheers, and loved him better than ever for his bravery. The King was so pleased that he presented his son with a tin badge, set with diamonds, on the back of which was engraved the picture of a Gigaboo.

Although Prince Jollikin was glad to be the hero of his nation, and enjoyed the triumph of having been able to conquer his ferocious enemy, he did not escape some inconvenience. For, as the result of his adventure, he found himself very stiff in the joints for several days after his fight with the Gigaboo.

THE NINTH SURPRISE

THE WIZARD AND THE PRINCESS

Within the depths of the mountains which bordered the Valley of Mo to the east lived a Wicked Wizard in a cavern of rubies. It was many, many feet below the surface of the earth and cut off entirely from the rest of the world, save for one passage which led through dangerous caves and tunnels to the top of the highest mountain. So that, in order to get out of his cavern, the Wizard was obliged to come to this mountain top, and from there descend to the outside world.

The Wizard lived all alone; but he did not mind that, for his thoughts were always on his books and studies, and he seldom showed himself on the surface of the earth. But when he did go out every one laughed at him; for this powerful magician was no taller than my knee, and was very old and wrinkled, so that he looked comical indeed beside an ordinary man.

The Wizard was nearly as sensitive as he was wicked, and was sorry he had not grown as big as other people; so the laughter that always greeted him made him angry.

At last he determined to find some magical compound that would make him grow bigger. He shut himself up in his cave and searched diligently amongst his books until, finally, he found a formula recommended by some dead and gone magician as sure to make any one grow a foot each day so long as the dose was taken. Most of the ingredients were quite easy

L. Frank Baum

to procure, being such as spiders' livers, kerosene oil and the teeth of canary birds, mixed together in a boiling caldron. But the last item of the recipe was so unusual that it made the Wizard scratch his head in perplexity.

It was the big toe of a young and beautiful princess.

The Wizard thought on the matter for three days, but nowhere could he think of a young and beautiful princess who would willingly part with her big toe—even that he might grow to be as big as he wished.

Then, as such a thing was not to be come by honestly, the Wicked Wizard resolved to steal it. So he went through all the caves and passages until he came to the mountain-top. Standing on the point of a rock he placed one hand on his chin and the other on the back of his neck, and then recited the following magical incantation:

"I wish to go
To steal the big toe
Of a princess I know,
In order to grow
Quite big. And so
I'll change, to a crow!"

No sooner had he spoken the words than he changed into a Black Crow, and flew away into the Valley of Mo, where he hid himself in a tall tree that grew near the King's palace.

That morning, as the Princess Truella was lying late in bed, with one of her dainty pink feet sticking out from under the covers, in through the window fluttered a Black Crow, which picked off her big toe and immediately flew away with it.

The Princess awoke with a scream and was horrified to find her beautiful foot ruined by the loss of her biggest toe. When the King and Queen and the Princes and Princesses, having heard her outcry, came running in to see what was the matter, they were each and all very indignant at the theft.

But, search as they might, nowhere could they find the audacious Black Crow, nor the Princess' big toe, and the whole court was in despair.

Finally Timtom, who was now a Prince, suggested that Truella seek assistance from the kind sorceress Maetta, who had helped him out of his own difficulties. The Princess thought well of this idea, and determined to undertake a journey to the castle.

She whistled for her favorite Stork, and soon the great bird came to her side. It was pure white, and of an extraordinary size. When the Stork had been saddled the Princess kissed her father and mother good by and seated herself on the bird's back, when it instantly rose into the air and flew away toward the castle of Maetta.

Traveling in this pleasant way, high in the air, the Princess crossed the River of Needles and the deep gulf and the dangerous wood, and at last was set down safe at the castle gates.

Maetta welcomed the pretty Princess very cordially and, on being told of her misfortune, at once agreed to assist her. So the sorceress consulted her Oracle, which told her truly anything she wanted to know, and then said to the Princess:

"Your toe is in the possession of the Wicked Wizard who lives in the ruby cave under the mountains. In order to recover it you must go yourself to seek it; but I warn you that the Wizard will put every obstacle in your path to prevent your finding the toe and taking it from him."

"Oh, dear!" exclaimed Truella, "I am afraid I shall never be able to get my toe from such a horrid man."

"Have courage, and trust in me," returned Maetta, "for I believe my powers are stronger than his. I shall now furnish

L. Frank Baum

you the weapons you must use to overcome him. Here is a magic umbrella, and in this basket which you must carry on your arm, you will find a lump of putty, an iron ball, a mirror, a package of chewing-gum and a magic veil, all of which will be very useful. Here, also, is a winged dagger, with which you must protect yourself if the Wizard attempts to harm you. With these enchanted weapons and a brave heart I believe you will succeed. So kiss me, my child, and start on your journey."

Truella thanked the kind sorceress, and mounting the saddle of her Stork flew away toward the high mountain in which dwelt the Wicked Wizard.

But the naughty man, by means of his black magic, saw her coming, and sent such a fierce wind to blow against her that it prevented the Stork from making any headway through the air. Therefore, in spite of his huge wings and remarkable strength, the brave bird was unable to get an inch nearer the mountain.

When Truella saw this she put up the umbrella and held it in front of the Stork; whereupon, being shielded from the wind, he flew easily to the mountain.

The Princess now dismounted and, looking into the hole at the top of the mountain, discovered a flight of stairs leading downward.

Taking her basket on her arm, as she had been directed, Truella walked boldly down the steps until she came to a door. But then she shrank back in affright, for before the door was coiled a great serpent, not quite a mile long and fully as large around as a stick of wood. The girl knew she must manage in some way to overcome this terrible creature, so when the serpent opened its mouth and raised its head to bite her, she reached within the basket, and finding the lump of putty, threw it quickly into the serpent's mouth. The creature snapped its jaws together so suddenly that its teeth stuck fast in the putty, and this made it so furious that it wriggled around until it had tied itself into a hard knot, and could wriggle no longer.

Seeing there was no further danger, the Princess passed the door and entered a large cave, which was but dimly lighted. While she paused to allow her eyes to become accustomed to the darkness, so she might see her way, a faint rustling sound reached her ears, and a moment later there came toward her a hideous old woman, lean and bent, with wrinkled face and piercing black eyes. She had only one tooth, but that was of enormous size, being nearly as large as the tusk of an elephant; and it curved out of her mouth and down under her chin, where it ended in a very sharp point. Her finger-nails were a foot long, and they, also, were very sharp and strong.

"What are you doing here?" asked the old woman, in a harsh voice, while she moved her horrible fingers, as if about to scratch out Truella's eyes.

"I came to see the Wizard," said the Princess, calmly, "and if you will allow me to pass I shall give you, in return for the favor, some delicious chewing-gum."

"Chewing-gum!" croaked the old woman, "what is that?"

"It is a dainty of which all ladies are very fond," replied Truella, taking the packet from her basket. "This is it."

The old woman hesitated a moment, and then said:

"Well, I'll try the chewing-gum and see what it is like; there will be plenty of time to scratch out your eyes afterwards."

She placed the gum in her mouth and tried to chew it, but when she shut her jaws together the great tusk went straight through her neck and came out at the back. The old hag gave a scream and put up her hands to pull out the tusk again, but so great was her excitement that in her haste she scratched out both her own eyes, and could no longer see where the Princess

L. Frank Baum

was standing.

So Truella ran through the cave and came to, a door, on which she knocked. Instantly it flew open, and before her she saw another cave, this time brightly lighted, but filled with knives and daggers, which were flying about in every direction. To enter this cave was impossible, for the Princess saw she would immediately be pierced by dozens of the sharp daggers. So she hesitated for a time, not knowing how to proceed; but, chancing to remember her basket, she took from it the iron ball, which she tossed into the center of the Cave of Daggers. At once the dangerous weapons began to strike against the ball, and as soon as they touched it they were broken and fell to the floor. In a short time every one of the knives and daggers had been spoiled by contact with the iron ball, and Truella passed safely through the cave and came to another long stairway leading downward. At the bottom of this she reached the third cave, and came upon a horrible monster.

It had the body of a zebra, the legs of a rhinoceros, the neck of a giraffe, the head of a bull dog, and three corrugated tails. This monster at once began to growl and run toward her, showing its terrible teeth and lashing its three tails. The Princess snatched the mirror from her basket and, as the creature came near her, she held the glittering surface before its eyes. It gave one look into the mirror and fell lifeless at her feet, being frightened to death by its own reflection in the mirror.

Truella now walked through several more caves and descended a long flight of stairs, which brought her to another door, on which was a sign that read:

"A. WIZARD, Esq.,
Office hours:
From 10:45 until
a quarter to 11."

The Princess, knowing that she had now reached the den of

the Wizard who had stolen her big toe, knocked boldly on the door.

"Come in!" called a voice.

Truella obeyed, and found herself in a large cave, the walls of which were lined with rubies. In each of the four corners were big electric lights, and these, shining upon the rubies, filled the cave with a deep red glow. The Wizard himself sat at his desk in one of the corners, and when the Princess entered he looked up and exclaimed:

"What! Is it you? Really, I did not expect to see you. How did you manage to pass the guards I placed within the caves and passageways to prevent your coming here?"

"Oh, that was not difficult," answered Truella, "for you must know I am protected by a power stronger than your own."

The Wizard was much annoyed at this reply, for he knew it was true, and that only by cunning could he hope to oppose the pretty Princess. Still, he was resolved not to give up the big toe unless obliged to, for it was necessary to complete the magic compound.

"What do you want?" he asked, after a moment's thought.

"I want the toe you stole from me while I was asleep."

The Wizard knew it was useless to deny the theft, so he replied:

"Very well; take a chair, and I will see if I can find it."

But Truella feared the little man was deceiving her; so when he turned his back she took the magic veil from her basket and threw it over her head. Immediately it began unfolding until it covered her completely, from head to foot.

L. Frank Baum

The Wizard walked over to a cupboard, which he opened; and, while pretending to search for the toe, he suddenly turned on a big faucet that was concealed under a shelf. At once the thunder rolled, the lightning flashed, and from the arched ceiling of the cavern drops of fire began to fall, coming thicker and thicker until a perfect shower of burning drops filled the room.

These fell hissing upon Truella's veil, but could not penetrate it, for they all bounded off and were scattered upon the rocky floor, where they soon burned themselves out. Seeing this the Wizard gave a sigh of disappointment and turned off the faucet, when the fire-drops ceased to fall.

"Please excuse this little interruption," he said, as if he had not been the cause of it himself. "I'll find the toe in a few minutes. I must have mislaid it somewhere."

But Truella suspected he was up to more mischief, and was on her guard. She saw him stealthily press a button, and in the same instant a deep gulf opened in the floor of the cave, half way between the Princess and the Wizard.

Truella did not know what this meant, at first, unless it was to prevent her getting across the room to where her toe was; but soon she noticed that the gulf was moving toward her, slowly, but steadily; and, as it extended across the cave from wall to wall, it would in time be sure to reach the spot where she stood, when she would, of course, fall into it.

When she saw her danger the Princess became frightened, and tried to escape through the door by which she had entered; but to her dismay she found it locked. Then she turned to look at the Wizard. The li ttle man had perched himself upon a high stool, and was carelessly swinging his feet and laughing with glee at Truella's awful peril. He thought that at last he had certainly found a way to destroy her. The poor Princess again looked into the gulf, which was gradually getting nearer and nearer; and she shuddered at its vast depths.

A cold wind began to sweep up from the abyss, and she heard mocking laughter and savage growls from below, as if evil spirits were eagerly waiting to seize her.

Just as she was giving way to despair, and the gulf had crept very close to her feet, Truella thought of her winged dagger. She drew it from her bosom and, pointing it toward her enemy, said:

"Save me from the Wizard's art—
Fly until you reach his heart.
Foil his power and set me free,
This is my command to thee!"

In a flash the dagger flew from her hand and struck the Wizard full on his breast. With a loud cry he fell forward into the gulf, which in the same instant closed up with a crash. Then, when the rocks about her had ceased trembling from the shock, the door swung open, leaving the Princess at liberty to go where she pleased.

She now searched the Wizard's cupboard until she found her toe, which had been safely hidden in a little ivory box. Truella stopped only long enough to put on her toe, and then she ran through the caves and up the stairways until she reached the top of the mountain again.

There she found her Stork patiently awaiting her and, having seated herself on its back, she rode safely and triumphantly back to her father's palace.

The King and Queen were delighted when she recounted to them the success of her adventure, but they shuddered when they learned of the fearful dangers their sweet little daughter had encountered.

"It seems to me," said the good Queen, "that a big toe is scarcely worth all the trouble you have had in recovering it."

"Perhaps not," replied the Princess, thoughtfully; "but a big toe is very handy to have when you wish to dance; and, after all, I succeeded in destroying the Wicked Wizard, which surely repays me for the trials I have been forced to undergo."

THE TENTH SURPRISE

THE DUCHESS BREDENBUTTA'S
VISIT TO TURVYLAND

The Duchess Bredenbutta was forty-seventh cousin to the Monarch of Mo and great-grandniece to the Queen; so you can readily see she was nearly related to the Princess Pattycake and had blue blood in her veins. She lived in a pretty house on the banks of Rootbeer River, and one of her favorite amusements was to row on the river in her boat, which, although rather small, was light as a cork.

One day, as usual, the Duchess went for a row on the river, expecting to return home in about an hour; but after floating a long distance down the stream she fell asleep in the boat and did not awake until she felt a sudden shock.

Then, sitting up and looking about her, she found, to her alarm, that the boat had drifted to the end of the Land of Mo, and was in the rapids leading to the Great Hole in the ground where the river disappeared from view. Becoming very much frightened, Bredenbutta looked for the oars of her boat, that she might row to the bank; but soon she discovered that the oars had fallen overboard and were lost, leaving her without any means of saving herself.

The poor Duchess now began to cry out; but no one heard her. Gradually the boat came nearer and nearer to the Great Hole, now bumping against the rocks and now spinning

L. Frank Baum

around with the current, until at last it paused for an instant on the very brink of the chasm down which the river fell.

The girl seized the sides of the boat in a firm grasp, and the next moment it plunged headlong into the Hole.

After the shock was over Bredenbutta wiped the moisture from her eyes and looked to see where she was, and what had become of her. She found that she had landed in a very remarkable country, and for a time could do nothing but gaze in wonder on the strange sights that met her view.

The trees were all growing on their top branches, with their roots high in the air; and the houses rested on the tops of their chimneys, the smoke going into the ground, and the doorsteps being at the tops of the buildings. A rabbit was flying around in the air, and a flock of skylarks walked on the ground, as if they belonged there.

Bredenbutta rubbed her eyes, for at first the girl thought she must be dreaming; but when she looked again everything was in the same unnatural position.

To add to her amazement she now saw a queer creature coming toward her. She might have taken him for a young man, only ho was just the reverse of any young man Bredenbutta had ever seen. He stood upon his hands, which were clad in boots, and used his feet as we use our hands, seeming to be very handy with his toes. His teeth were in his ears, and he ate with them and heard with his mouth. He also smelled with his eyes and saw out of his nose—which was all very curious. When he walked he ran, and when he ran he stood still. He spoke when he was silent and remained dumb when he had anything to say. In addition to this, he wept real tears when he was pleased, and laughed merrily whenever anything grieved him.

It was no wonder the Duchess Bredenbutta stared in surprise when such an odd creature came up to her backward and looked at her solemnly from his pug nose.

"Who are you?" asked Bredenbutta, as soon as she could find breath to speak.

The young man kept quiet and answered: "My name is Upsydoun."

"I think you are," laughed Bredenbutta.

"You think I am what?" demanded the young man, the voice coming from his ear.

"Up-side-down," she replied.

At this retort the tears rolled down his cheeks with joy.

"Why, it is *you* who are up-side-down," he said; "how in the world did you get up here?"

"Down here, you mean," corrected the Duchess, with dignity.

"I mean nothing of the kind," he said, silently, while his nose twinkled with amusement; "this country is up, and not down."

"What country is it?" inquired Bredenbutta, much perplexed by such an absurd statement.

"Why, Turvyland, to be sure," was the answer.

"Oh!" sighed Bredenbutta; but she was no wiser than before.

"Now you are here," said Upsydoun, "you may come home with me and eat some dinner."

"I shall be very glad to," answered the Duchess, who was really hungry. "Where do you live?"

"Over there," replied Upsydoun, pointing to the south; "so

stay where you are and follow me." Then he walked away on his hands in exactly the opposite direction from that he had indicated.

Bredenbutta followed him, and shortly after encountered several other people, of just the same queer appearance as her conductor. They looked out of their noses at her in great surprise, and, without speaking, asked Upsydoun who she was.

"The Duchess Bredenbutta," he silently answered, "I found her where the Rootbeer River bubbles up. Isn't she a queer-looking creature?"

"She is, indeed," they all answered, in a still chorus, and then they followed the girl out of curiosity, as boys follow a band or a dancing bear. When they reached the house of Upsydoun more than a hundred inhabitants of Turvyland were at Bredenbutta's heels and Upsydoun's thumbs.

She was welcomed very kindly, however, and the young man's mother kissed the Duchess with her left ear, an act which was considered a special mark of favor in Turvyland,

"Would you like to stand up and rest yourself until dinner-time?" asked the lady when the girl had entered the parlor.

"No, thank you," replied Bredenbutta, who was very tired. Being ignorant of their customs she did not know these people usually stood up when they slept or rested. Her answer seemed to satisfy Upsydoun's mother, who thought when she said "no" she meant "yes."

"You really don't look equal to lying down," she remarked, pleasantly; "so you may stand until I call you to dinner, which will be in a long time." Then she excused herself and walked backward out of the window,which Bredenbutta noticed they all used instead of doors.

"Dear me," said the Duchess, when she was left alone; "I am

sure I shall never be able to understand these strange people. But I mean to sit down, anyway, and if it really is a long time before dinner, I shall probably starve in the meantime."

She had not rested more than a few minutes, however, before the lady again put her foot through the window, and waving it invitingly toward her exclaimed: "Go away to dinner."

"Go away!" replied the Duchess in dismay; "where shall I go to?"

"Why, to me, of course," answered Upsydoun's mother, dumbly; but she winked her nose thoughtfully, as if she scarcely knew how to converse with her strange visitor. Surely Bredenbutta ought to know that when they said "go" in Turvyland, they meant "come."

In spite of her uncertainty, she followed her hostess, and when they entered the dining-room the Duchess was shocked to see all the family stand on their heads on the chairs and pick up their knives and forks with their toes. She was more horrified, however, when they began to eat; for, contrary to all custom, these people placed their food in their ears. And they did it so calmly that she did not even remonstrate, remembering it must be their habit to eat in this way.

She, herself, sat down in her chair in a proper manner, and began to eat with the fork in her hand; and when the people of Turvyland saw this, they all shed tears of merriment.

Just then the youngest child of the family began laughing, and the mother rushed to it as fast as her hands could carry her, to see what was the matter. But the child had only put its foot into its pocket and could not get it out again. The mother soon managed to get it free, and then the child stopped laughing and began weeping as happily as any of the others.

Bredenbutta was greatly bewildered at all this, but she ate heartily, nevertheless, and after having begged her in vain to stand on her head, as they did, the family let her alone, being surprised to see how well she could use her hands. After dinner Upsydoun's sister played on the piano with her toes, while the others indulged in a dance, whirling around on their thumbs in a manner truly marvelous, and seeming, by their tears, to enjoy themselves very much.

As the dance ended a kitten came running into the room on its ears and the tip of its tail, and this looked so funny that Bredenbutta began laughing. But seeing she had frightened her kind friends, who wanted to send for a doctor, she refrained from laughing, and asked, gravely, if she could not find a way to return to the Valley of Mo.

"The only possible way of getting down there," replied Upsydoun, "is to jump into the Rootbeer River; but that would be dangerous, and none of our people have ever tried it"

"Any danger," said the Duchess, "I will gladly brave; for otherwise I shall be obliged to spend my entire life down here, among people whose ways are exactly opposite to my own. If you will kindly take me to the river I shall lose no time in making an effort to return home."

They good-naturedly assented to this, and walked backward with her until they came to the place where the river bubbled up. It really did bubble *up*, Bredenbutta noticed, although she knew very well she had fallen *down* the Great Hole. But, then, everything was topsyturvy in this strange land.

The girl found her little boat, which had stranded on the beach, and having placed it where she could push it into the river, she turned to say good by to the queer people of Turvyland.

"I am glad to see you go," said Upsydoun, without speaking, "for I like you. But you are a strange creature, and perhaps know what is best for you. Here are some oars for your boat, for I see you have none, and when you get down to your country you may need them."

Bredenbutta joyfully accepted the oars, and placed them in her boat. Then the people of Turvyland all kissed her with their left ears and waved their toes in farewell, while the Duchess got into the boat and pushed it out into the river.

Instantly she was in the midst of such a whirling of foam and rushing and roaring of rootbeer that she could neither see nor hear anything. Gasping for breath, the girl clung tightly to the sides of the boat, and in a few minutes it was all over, and the boat bobbed up in the Valley of Mo—just above the Great Hole. Bredenbutta then seized the oars and rowed hard until there was no danger of her falling in again, and soon she had passed the rapids and was rowing safely up the river to her own home.

Of course the Duchess was very glad again to be among the people who acted in a natural manner, instead of the absurd fashion of her friends, the Turvylanders. She resolved that whenever she rowed her boat upon the river again, she would be careful to keep away from the Great Hole, for she realized that another visit to Upsydoun and his people would be very trying to her nerves.

L. Frank Baum

THE ELEVENTH SURPRISE

PRINCE FIDDLECUMDOO AND THE GIANT

It happened, one morning, that the Monarch of Mo was not in his usual pleasant humor; and, of course, there was an excellent reason for this.

At the back of his garden grew one tree that generally bore an abundant crop of animal-crackers, and although the King and his court, being surfeited with all the dainties of the land, did not care much for these edibles, the younger inhabitants of Mo were especially fond of them, and yelled with delight whenever the King divided the crop of his tree among them.

A few days before the King had examined the tree and found the animal-crackers not quite ripe. Whereupon he had gone away and forgotten all about them. And, in his absence, they had ripened to a delicious light brown; and their forms had rounded out, so that they hung as thickly together as peas in a pod. As they swung from their stems, swaying backward and forward in the light breeze, they waited and waited for some one to come and pick them. But no one came near the tree, and the animals grew cross and restless in consequence.

"I wonder when we shall be gathered," remarked a hippopotamus-cracker, with a yawn.

"Oh, you wonder, do you?" mockingly replied a camel-cracker hanging near, "do you really expect any one to gather *you*, with your thick hide and clumsy legs? Why, the children would break their teeth on you at the first bite."

"What!" screamed the hippopotamus, in much anger, "do you dare insult *me*, you humpbacked beast of burden?"

"Now then—now then!" interrupted a wolf-cracker that hung from a stem just above them; "what's the use of fighting, when we are so soon to be eaten?"

But the camel-cracker would not be appeased.

"Thick-headed brute!" he yelled at the hippopotamus, angrily.

"Hump-backed idiot!" shrieked the other.

At this the camel swung himself fiercely on his branch, and bumped against the hippopotamus, knocking him off from the tree. The ground underneath was chocolate, and it was soft and sticky, not having dried since the last rain. So when the hippopotamus fell he sank half way into the ground, and his beautiful brown color was spattered with the muddy chocolate.

At this vengeful deed on the part of the camel all the other animals became furious. A full-grown goat-cracker swung himself against the camel and knocked it, in turn, from its stem; and in falling on the ground it broke its hump off. Then a lion-cracker knocked the goat down, and an elephant knocked a cat down, and soon the whole tree was in a violent commotion. The animals fought with each other so desperately that before long the entire treeful of animal-crackers had fallen to the ground, where many lay broken and disfigured, and the remainder were sunk deep in the chocolate mud.

So when the King, finally remembering his tree, came and looked on the sorry sight, it dampened his usual good spirits, and he heartily wished he had picked the quarrelsome crackers before they began to fight among themselves.

　　　　　L. Frank Baum

While he stood thinking dismally on this, up came Prince Fiddlecumdoo and asked permission to go on a journey.

"Where do you wish to go?" asked the King.

"I am tired of this beautiful Valley," answered Fiddlecumdoo, "and as the bicycle tree beside the Crystal Lake is now hanging full of ripe wheels, I thought I would gather one and ride over into the next valley in search of adventure." You see, this Prince was the King's youngest son, and had been rather spoiled by petting, as youngest sons often are.

"The next valley, my son, is inhabited by the giant Hartilaf," said the King, "and should you meet him he might do you an injury."

"Oh, I am not afraid of Hartilaf," replied Fiddlecumdoo, boldly. "If he should not be pleasant to me, I could run away from him on my wheel."

"I don't know about that," responded the King. "There may be bicycle trees in the next valley, as well as here; and it is always dangerous and foolish for any one to leave this Valley, where there is everything that heart could wish. Instead of running away in search of adventures, you would do better to remain at home and help your mother pick collar buttons and neckties for the family."

"That is work," said Fiddlecumdoo, sulkily, "and I hate work."

"Yet somebody has to pick the collar buttons," returned the King, "or we should be unable to keep our collars on."

"Then let Jollikin help my mother. I am horribly tired of this stupid place, and shall not be happy until I have traveled around and seen something more of the world."

"Well, well! go if you wish," answered the King, impatiently. "But take care of yourself, for when you are away from this

Valley there will be no one to protect you from danger."

"I can take care of myself," cried the Prince, "so do not worry about me," and he ran away quickly, before his father had time to change his mind and withdraw his consent.

He selected the best and ripest bicycle on the tree, and, having mounted it, was soon speeding away along the path to the mountains.

When he reached the far eastern part of Mo he came on a bush bearing a very good quality of violins, and this at once attracted Fiddlecumdoo, who was a most excellent violinist, being able to play correctly a great number of tunes. So he dismounted and selected from the bush a small violin that seemed to have a sweet tone. This he carried with him, under his arm, thinking if he became lonesome he could amuse himself with the music.

Shortly after resuming his journey he came to the Maple Plains, a level stretch of country composed entirely of maple sugar. These plains were quite smooth, and very pleasant to ride on; but so swiftly did his bicycle carry him that he soon crossed the plains and came on a river of pure maple syrup, so wide and deep that he could neither leap nor swim it.

Dismounting from his bicycle the Prince began looking for some means of crossing the river. No bridge was visible in either direction, and the bank was bare save for a few low bushes on which grew maple bonbons and maple caramels.

But Prince Fiddlecumdoo did not mean to be turned back by so small a matter as a river, so he scooped a hole in the maple sand, and having filled it with syrup from the river, lighted a match and began boiling it. After it had boiled for a time the maple syrup became stringy, and the Prince quickly threw a string of it across the river. It hardened almost immediately, and on this simple bridge the Prince rode over the stream.

Once on the other side he sped up the mountain and over the top into the next valley, where, he stopped and began to look about him.

He could see no roads in any direction, but away down at the foot of the valley was a monstrous house, so big you could easily put a small village inside it, including the church. This, Fiddlecumdoo thought, must be where the giant lived; and, although he saw no one about the house, he decided to make a call and introduce himself to Mr. Hartilaf. So he rode slowly down the valley, playing on his violin as he went, that the music might announce his coming.

The giant Hartilaf was lying on the sofa in his sitting-room, waiting for his wife to prepare the dinner; and he had nearly fallen asleep when the sound of Fiddlecumdoo's music fell on his ear. This was so unusual in his valley that the giant arose and went to the front door to see what caused it.

The Prince had by this time nearly reached the house, and when the giant appeared he was somewhat startled, as he had not expected to see any one quite so big. But he took care not to show any fear, and, taking off his hat, he bowed politely to the giant and said:

"This is Mr. Hartilaf, I suppose?"

"That is my name," replied the giant, grinning at the small size of his visitor. "May I ask who you are?"

"I am Prince Fiddlecumdoo, and I live in the next valley, which is called the Valley of Mo. Being determined to see something of the world, I am traveling for pleasure, and have just dropped in on you for a friendly call."

"You are very welcome, I am sure," returned the giant. "If you will graciously step into my humble home I shall be glad to entertain you at dinner."

Prince Fiddlecumdoo bowed low and accepted the invitation, but when he endeavored to enter the house he found the steps so big that even the first one was higher than his head, and he could not climb to the top of it.

Seeing his difficulty the giant carefully picked him up with one finger and his thumb, and put him down on the palm of his other hand.

"Do not leave my bicycle," said the Prince, "for should anything happen to it I could not get home again."

So the giant put the bicycle in his vest pocket, and then he entered the house and walked to the kitchen, where his wife was engaged preparing the dinner.

"Guess what I've found," said the giant to his wife, holding his hand doubled up so she could not see the Prince.

"I'm sure I don't know," answered the woman.

"But, guess!" pleaded the giant.

"Go away and don't bother me," she replied, bending over the stewpan, "or you won't have any dinner to-day."

The giant, however, was in a merry mood, and for a joke he suddenly opened his hand and dropped the Prince down his wife's neck.

"Oh, oh!" she screamed, trying to get at the place where the Prince had fallen, which was near the small of her back. "What is it? I'm sure it's some horrible crocodile, or dragon, or something that will bite me!" And the poor woman lay down on the carpet and began to kick her heels against the floor in terror.

The giant roared with laughter, but the Prince, now being able to crawl out, scrambled from the lady's neck, and, standing

L. Frank Baum

beside her head, he made a low bow and said:

"Do not be afraid, Madam; it is only I. But I must say it was a very ungallant trick for your husband to play on you, to say nothing of my feelings in the matter."

"So it was," she exclaimed, getting upon her feet again, and staring curiously at Fiddlecumdoo. "But tell me who you are and where you came from."

The giant, having enjoyed his laugh, now introduced the Prince to his wife, and as dinner was ready to serve they sat down at the table together.

Fiddlecumdoo got along very well at dinner, for the giant thoughtfully placed him on the top of the table, where he could walk around as he pleased. There being no knife nor fork small enough for him to use, the Prince took one of the giant's toothpicks, which was as big as a sword, and with this served himself from the various dishes that stood on the table.

When the meal was over the giant lighted his pipe, the bowl of which was as big as a barrel, and asked Fiddlecumdoo if he would kindly favor them with some music.

"Certainly," replied the Prince.

"Please come into the kitchen," said the giantess, "for then I can listen to the music while I am washing the dishes."

The prince did not like to refuse this request, although at home he was not allowed to enter his mother's kitchen; so the giant carried him in and placed him on a high shelf, where Fiddlecumdoo seated himself on a spool of thread and began to play his violin.

The big people enjoyed the music very much at first, for the Prince was a capital player. But soon came a disagreeable interruption.

About a month before the giant had caught several dancing-bears in the mountains, and, having brought them home, had made them into strings of sausages. These were hanging in graceful festoons from the beams of the kitchen ceiling, awaiting the time when they should be eaten.

Now when the dancing-bear sausages heard the music of Fiddlecumdoo's violin, they could not resist dancing; for it is well known that sausages made from real dancing-bears can not remain quiet where there is music. The Prince was playing such a lively tune, that presently the strings of sausage broke away from the ceiling and fell clattering to the floor, where they danced about furiously. Not being able to see where they were going, they bumped against the giant and his wife, thumping them on their heads and backs, and pounding them so severely that the woman became frightened and hid under the table, while the giant started to run away.

Seeing their plight, Fiddlecumdoo stopped playing, and at once the sausages fell to the floor and lay still.

"That was strange," said the giant, as soon as he could catch his breath; "the bears evidently do not forget how to dance even after they are chopped up into sausage meat. I must beg you to abandon your concert for the present, but before you visit us again we shall have eaten the sausages, and then you may play to your heart's content."

"Had I known they were so lively," remarked the giantess, as she crawled from beneath the table, "we should have eaten them before this."

"That reminds me that I intended to have stewed polar bears for supper," continued the giant; "so I think I will walk over into Alaska and catch some."

"Perhaps the Prince would prefer elephant pie," suggested the lady, "and in that case you might make a run into South America for elephants."

"I have no choice in the matter," said the Prince, "never having eaten either. But is it not rather a long journey to Alaska or to South America?"

"Not at all!" protested the giant. "I shall enjoy the walk, and can easily be back by sundown. Won't you come with me?" he asked the boy. But Fiddlecumdoo did not like the idea of so long a journey, and begged to be excused.

The giantess brought her lord a great bag to put the polar bears in, and he prepared to start.

"I leave you to amuse my wife during my absence," he said to the Prince. "Pray make yourself entirely at home, and use my castle as you would your own house, and if I have good luck you shall eat a delicious polar-bear stew for your supper."

Then he slung the sack across his back and went away, whistling merrily. And so great were his strides that in less than a minute he was out of sight.

"This is my busy day," said the giantess to Fiddlecumdoo, "and I fear I shall not be able to entertain you in a proper manner, for I must hasten to the laundry to wash the clothes. However, if you care to accompany me, we may converse together while I am doing my work."

"I shall take great pleasure in visiting your laundry," he replied, "for never before have I been in such a place. And surely it will be more agreeable to watch you at your work than to spend the day alone in these great rooms."

"Come along, then," she said, and picking him up she placed him in the pocket of her apron, for she knew he would be unable to walk down the flight of stairs that led to the laundry. He was very comfortable in the pocket, which was just deep enough to allow his head and shoulders to project from the top. Therefore he was able to see all that was going on while the lady was at work. He watched her wash and rinse the clothes, and was greatly interested in the operation, as it was all new to him.

By and by the giantess brought an immense clothes-wringer from a shelf, and having fastened it to the side of the big wash tub began to wring out the clothes.

Prince Fiddlecumdoo had never seen a clothes-wringer before, and so pleased was he with the novelty of it that he leaned far out of the pocket to watch it work. But, unfortunately, he lost his balance, and before he knew what had happened to him had fallen from the pocket and lay sprawling on one of the giant's shirts, which was just then passing through the wringer.

The woman did not notice his fall, and the next instant he was drawn between the two great rollers, and came out on the other side as thin and flat as a sheet of paper.

Then the giant's wife saw what she had done, and realizing how serious was the Prince's condition, the good lady was much grieved over the accident. She picked Fiddlecumdoo up and tried to stand him on his feet, but he was so thin that at the least draft he fluttered like a flag, while a puff of wind would blow him completely over.

"Dear me!" exclaimed the woman, sorrowfully, "whatever can we do with you in that shape?"

"I really do not know what will become of me," replied the Prince. "I am certainly no good in this condition. I can not even walk across the room without toppling over. Can not you manage to push me together again?" The giantess tried to do this, but the Prince was so sharp that his edges hurt her hands, and all she could do was to fold him up and carry him into the drawing-room, where she laid him carefully on the center-table.

Just before sundown the giant returned from Alaska, bringing several fat polar-bears in his bag; and scarcely had he set foot within the house before he inquired after his guest, the Prince.

"You will find him on the drawing-room table," said the giantess. "I accidently ran him through the clothes-wringer this afternoon, and the poor boy is as thin as a pie crust. So I folded him up and put him away until you returned."

The giant immediately went to the table and unfolded Fiddlecumdoo, asking him how he felt.

"Very miserable," answered the Prince, "for I can not move at all when I am folded up. Where is my bicycle?"

The giant searched all his pockets, but could not find it.

"I must have lost it on my journey to Alaska," he said.

"Then how am I ever to get home again?" asked the Prince.

"That is a puzzle," the giant responded, thoughtfully. "I do not see how you could ride on a bicycle even if you had one, and you certainly can not walk far in your present condition."

"Not if the wind blows," acknowledged the Prince.

"Couldn't you go edgewise?" asked the giant after a moment's reflection.

"I might try," answered Fiddlecumdoo, hopefully.

So the giant stood him up, and he tried to walk edgewise. But whenever a breath of wind struck him he fell over at once, and several times he got badly crumpled up, so that the giant had to smooth him out again with his hands.

"This certainly will not do at all," declared the giant; "for not only are you getting wrinkled, but you are liable to be blown away; altogether. I have just thought of a plan to get you back into the Valley of Mo again, and when you are in your own country your friends may get you out of the scrape the best way they can."

Hartilaf then made the Prince into a neat roll and tied a string around the middle, to hold it in place. Then he tucked the roll under his arm and carried it to the top of the mountain that stood between the two valleys. Placing the Prince carefully on the ground he started him rolling, and in a short time he had rolled down the mountain side into the Valley of Mo.

At first the people were much frightened, not knowing what this strange thing could be that had come rolling into their midst. They stood around, curiously looking at the roll, but afraid to touch it, when suddenly Fiddlecumdoo began to cry out. And then, so fearful was the sound, they all ran away as fast as their legs could carry them.

Prince Thinkabit, however, being more courageous than the rest, at last ventured to approach and cut the string that fastened the roll. Instantly it opened, and to their amazement the people saw what it was.

"Upon my word, it is brother Fiddlecumdoo!" cried Prince Thinkabit. "The giant must have stepped on him."

"No, indeed," said poor Fiddlecumdoo, "I've been run through a clothes-wringer, which is much worse than being stepped on."

With many expressions of pity the kind people stood the Prince up and helped him to the palace, where the King was greatly shocked at his sad plight. Fiddlecumdoo was so broad that the only thing he could sit down on was the sofa, and he was so thin that when Princess Pattycake sneezed he was blown half way across the room.

At dinner he could eat nothing that was not sliced as thin as a shaving, and so sad was his predicament that the King determined to ask the Wise Donkey what could be done to

L. Frank Baum

relieve his unfortunate son.

After hearing all the particulars of the accident, the Donkey said: "Blow him up."

"I did blow him up, for being so careless," replied the King; "but it didn't make him any thicker."

"What I mean," explained the Donkey, "is to bore a hole in the top of his head, and blow air into him until he resumes his natural shape. Then, if he takes care of himself, he soon will be all right again."

So the King returned to the palace and bored a hole in Fiddlecumdoo's head, and then pumped him full of air with a bicycle pump. When he had filled out into his natural shape they put a plug in the hole, and stopped it up; and after that Fiddlecumdoo could walk around as well as before his accident.

His only danger now was that he might get punctured; and, indeed, his friends found him one day lying in the garden, all flattened out again, the Prince having pricked his finger on a rose-bush and thereby allowed his air to escape. But they inflated him once again, and afterward he was more careful of himself.

Fiddlecumdoo had such a horror of being flat that, if his father ever wished to make him behave, he threatened to stick a pin into him, and that always had the desired effect.

After several years, the Prince, being a hearty eater, filled up with solid flesh, and had no further use for the air-pump; but his experience had made him so nervous that he never again visited the giant Hartilaf, for fear of encountering another accident.

THE TWELFTH SURPRISE

THE LAND OF THE CIVILIZED MONKEYS

I must now tell you of a very strange adventure that befell Prince Zingle, which, had it not turned out exactly as it did, might have resulted in making him a captive for life in a remarkable country.

By consulting Smith's History of Prince Zingle you will notice that from boyhood he had a great passion for flying kites, and unlike other boys, he always undertook to make each kite larger than the last one. Therefore his kites grew in size, and became larger and larger, until at length the Prince made one twice as tall as himself.

When it was finished he was very proud of this great kite, and took it out to a level place to see how well it would fly, being accompanied by many of the people of Mo, who took considerable interest in the Prince's amusement.

There happened to be a strong south wind blowing and, fearing the kite might get away from him, Zingle tied the string around his waist. It flew beautifully at first, but pulled so hard the Prince could scarcely hold it.

At last, when the string was all let out, there came a sudden gust of wind, and in an instant poor Zingle was drawn into the air as easily as an ordinary kite draws its tail. Up and up he soared, and the kite followed the wind and carried him over

L. Frank Baum

many countries until the strength died out of the air, when the kite slowly settled toward the earth and landed the Prince in the top of a tall tree.

He now untied the string from his waist and fastened it to a branch of the tree, as he did not wish to lose the kite after all his bother in making it.

Then he began to climb down to the ground, but on reaching the lower branches he was arrested by a most curious sight.

Standing on the ground, and gazing up at him, were a dozen monkeys, all very neatly dressed and all evidently filled with surprise at the Prince's sudden appearance in the tree.

"What a very queer animal!" exclaimed an old monkey, who wore a tall silk hat and had white kid gloves on his hands. Gold spectacles rested on his nose, and he pointed toward the Prince with a gold-headed cane. By his side was a little girl-monkey, dressed in pink skirts and a blue bonnet; and when she saw Zingle she clung to the old monkey's hand and seemed frightened.

"Oh, grandpapa!" she cried; "take me back to mamma; I'm afraid the strange beast will bite me."

Just then a big monkey, wearing a blue coat with brass buttons and swinging a short club in his hand, strutted up to them and said:

"Don't be afraid, little one. The beast can't hurt you while I'm around!" And then he tipped his cap over his left ear and shook his club at the Prince, as if he did not know what fear meant.

Two monkeys, who were dressed in red jackets and carried muskets in their hands, now came running up, and, having looked at Zingle with much interest, they called for some one to bring them a strong rope.

"We will capture the brute and put him in the Zoo," said one of the soldier-monkeys.

"What kind of animal is it?" asked the other.

"I do not know. But some of our college professors can doubtless tell, and even if they can't they will give it some scientific name that will satisfy the people just as well."

All this time Prince Zingle remained clinging to the branches of the tree. He could not understand a word of the monkey language, and therefore had no idea what they were talking about; but he judged from their actions that the monkeys were not friendly. When they brought a long and stout rope, and prepared to throw one end of it over his head, in order to capture him, he became angry and called out to them:

"Stop—I command you! What is the meaning of this strange conduct? I am Prince Zingle, eldest son of the Monarch of Mo, and, since I have been blown into your country through an accident, I certainly deserve kind treatment at your hands."

But this speech had no meaning in the ears of the monkeys, who said to each other:

"Hear him bark! He jabbers away almost as if he could talk!"

By this time a large crowd of monkeys had surrounded the tree, some being barefooted boy-monkeys, and some lady-monkeys dressed in silken gowns and gorgeous raiment of the latest mode, and others men-monkeys of all sorts and conditions. There were dandified monkeys and sober-looking business monkeys, as well as several who appeared to be politicians and officials of high degree.

"Stand back, all of you!" shouted one of the soldiers. "We're going to capture this remarkable beast for the royal menagerie, and unless you stand out of the way he may show fight and bite some one."

L. Frank Baum

So they moved back to a safe distance, and the soldier-monkey prepared to throw a rope.

"Stop!" cried Zingle, again; "do you take me for a thief, that you try to bind me? I am a prince of the royal blood, and unless you treat me respectfully I shall have my father, the King, march his army on you and destroy your whole country."

"He barks louder," said the soldier. "Look out for him; he may be dangerous." The next moment he threw the rope and caught poor Zingle around his arms and body, so that he was helpless. Then the soldier-monkey pulled hard on the rope, and Prince Zingle fell out of the tree to the ground.

At first the monkeys all pressed backward, as if frightened, but their soldiers cried out:

"We've got him; he can't bite now."

Then one of them approached the Prince and punched him with a stick, saying, "Stand up!"

Zingle did not understand the words, but he resented being prodded with the stick, so he sprang up and rushed on the soldier, kicking the stick from his hands, his own arms being bound by the rope.

The monkeys screamed and rushed in every direction, but the other soldier came behind the Prince and knocked him down with the butt of his gun. Then he tied his legs with another rope, and, seeing him thus bound, the crowd of monkeys, which had scattered and fallen over one another in their efforts to escape, came creeping timidly back, and looked on him with fear and trembling.

"We've subdued him at last," remarked the soldier who had been kicked. "But he's a very fierce animal, and I shall take him to the Zoo and lock him in one of the strongest cages."

So they led poor Zingle away to where the Royal Zoological Gardens were located, and there they put him into a big cage with iron bars, the door being fastened with two great padlocks.

Before very long every monkey in the country learned that a strange beast had been captured and brought to the Zoo; and soon a large crowd had gathered before Zingle's cage to examine him.

"Isn't he sweet!" said a lady-monkey who held a green parasol over her head and wore a purple veil on her face.

"Sweet!" grunted a man-monkey standing beside her, "he's the ugliest looking brute I ever saw! Scarcely has any hair on him at all, and no tail, and very little chin. I wonder where on earth the creature came from?"

"It may be one of those beings from whom our race is descended," said another onlooker. "The professors say we evolved from some primitive creature of this sort."

"Heaven forbid!" cried a dandy-monkey, whose collar was so high that it kept tipping his hat over his eyes. "If I thought such a creature as that was one of my forefathers, I should commit suicide at once."

Zingle had been sitting on the floor of his cage and wondering what was to become of him in this strange country of monkeys, and now, to show his authority, one of the keepers took a long stick and began to poke the Prince to make him stand up.

"Stop that!" shouted the angry captive, and catching hold of the stick he jerked it from the keeper's hand and struck him a sharp blow on the head with it.

All the lady-monkeys screamed at this, and the men-monkeys exclaimed:

L. Frank Baum

"What an ugly disposition the beast has!"

The children-monkeys began to throw peanuts between the bars of the cage, and Zingle, who had now become very hungry, picked them up and ate them. This act so pleased the little monkeys that they shouted with laughter.

At last two solemn-looking monkeys with gray hair, and wearing long black coats and white neckties, came up to the cage, where they were greeted with much respect by the other monkeys.

"So this is the strange animal," said one of the new-comers, putting on his spectacles and looking sharply at the captive; "do you recognize the species, Professor?"

The other aged monkey also regarded the Prince critically before he answered:

"I can not say I have ever seen a specimen of this genus before. But one of our text-books mentions an obscure animal called Homo Peculiaris, and I have no doubt this is one of that family. I shall write an article on the creature and claim he is a Homo, and without doubt the paper will create quite a stir in the scientific world."

"See here," suddenly demanded Prince Zingle, standing up and shaking the bars of his cage, "are you going to give me anything to eat? Or do you expect me to live on peanuts forever?"

Not knowing what he said, none of the monkeys paid any attention to this question. But one of the professor-monkeys appeared to listen attentively, and remarked to friend: "There seems to be a smoothness and variety of sound in his speech that indicates that he possesses some sort of language. Had I time to study this brute, I might learn his method of communicating with his fellows. Indeed, there is a possibility that he may turn out to be the missing link."

However, the professor not yet having learned his language, Prince Zingle was obliged to remain hungry. The monkeys threw several cocoanuts into the cage, but the prisoner did not know what kind of fruit these were; so, after several attempts to bite the hard shell, he decided they were not good to eat.

Day after day now passed away, and, although crowds of monkeys came to examine Zingle in his cage, the poor Prince grew very pale and thin for lack of proper food, while the continuance of his unhappy imprisonment made him sad and melancholy.

"Could I but escape and find my way back to my father's valley," he moaned, wearily, "I should be willing to fly small kites forever afterward."

Often he begged them to let him go, but the monkeys gruffly commanded him to "stop his jabbering," and poked him with long sticks having sharp points; so that the Prince's life became one of great misery.

At the end of about two weeks a happy relief came to Zingle, for then a baby hippopotamus was captured and brought to the Royal Zoo, and after this the monkeys left the Prince's cage and crowded around that of the new arrival.

Finding himself thus deserted, Prince Zingle began to seek a means of escape from his confinement. His first attempt was to break the iron bars; but soon he found they were too big and strong. Then he shook the door with all his strength; but the big padlocks held firm, and could not be broken. Then the prisoner gave way to despair, and threw himself on the floor of the cage, weeping bitterly.

Suddenly he heard a great shout from the direction of the cage where the baby hippopotamus was confined, and, rising to his feet, the Prince walked to the bars and attempted to look out and discover what was causing the excitement. To his astonishment he found he was able to thrust his head between

L. Frank Baum

two of the iron bars, having grown so thin through hunger and abuse, that he was much smaller than when the monkeys had first captured him. He realized at once that if his head would pass between the bars, his body could be made to do so, likewise. So he struggled bravely, and at last succeeded in squeezing his body between the bars and leaping safely to the ground.

Finding himself at liberty, the Prince lost no time in running to the tree where he had left his kite. But on the way some of the boy-monkeys discovered him and raised a great cry, which soon brought hundreds of his enemies in pursuit.

Zingle had a good start, however, and soon reached the tree. Quickly he climbed up the trunk and branches until he had gained the limb where the string of his kite was still fastened. Untying the cord, he wound it around his waist several times, and then, finding a strong north wind blowing, he skilfully tossed the kite into the air. At once it filled and mounted to the sky, lifting Zingle from the tree and carrying him with perfect ease.

It was fortunate he got away at that moment, for several of the monkeys had scrambled up the tree after him, and were almost near enough to seize him by the legs when, to their surprise, he shot into the air. Indeed, so amazed were they by this remarkable escape of their prisoner that the monkeys remained staring into the air until Prince Zingle had become a little speck in the sky above them and finally disappeared.

That was the last our Prince ever saw of the strange country of the monkeys, for the wind carried his kite straight back to the Valley of Mo. When Zingle found himself above his father's palace, he took out his pocket-knife and cut the string of the kite, and immediately fell head foremost into a pond of custard that lay in the back yard, where he dived through a floating island of whipped cream and disappeared from view.

Nuphsed, who was sitting on the bank of the custard lake, was nearly frightened into fits by this sight; and he ran to tell the King that a new meteor had fallen and ruined one of his floating islands.

Thereupon the monarch and several of his courtiers rushed out and found Prince Zingle swimming ashore; and the King was so delighted at seeing his lost son again that he clasped him joyfully in his arms.

The next moment he regretted this act, for his best ermine robe was smeared its whole length with custard, and would need considerable cleaning before it would be fit to wear again.

The Prince and the King soon changed their clothes, and then there was much rejoicing throughout the land. Of course the first thing Zingle asked for was something to eat, and before long he was sitting at a table heaped with all sorts of good things, plucked fresh from the trees.

The people crowded around him, demanding the tale of his adventures, and their surprise was only equaled by their horror when they learned he had been captured by a band of monkeys, and shut up in a cage because he was thought to be a dangerous wild beast.

Experience is said to be an excellent teacher, although a very cruel one. Prince Zingle had now seen enough of foreign countries to remain contented with his own beautiful Valley, and, although it was many years before he again attempted to fly a kite, it was noticed that, when he at last did indulge in that sport, the kite was of a very small size.

L. Frank Baum

THE THIRTEENTH SURPRISE

THE STOLEN PLUM-PUDDING

The King's plum-pudding crop had for some time suffered from the devastations of a secret enemy. Each day, as he examined the vines, he found more and more of the plum-pudding missing, and finally the monarch called his Wise Men together and asked them what he should do.

The Wise Men immediately shut their eyes and pondered so long over the problem that they fell fast asleep. While they slept still more of the plum-pudding was stolen. When they awoke the King was justly incensed, and told the Wise Men that unless they discovered the thief within three days he would give them no cake with their ice-cream.

This terrible threat at last aroused them to action, and, after consulting together, they declared that in their opinion it was the Fox that had stolen the pudding.

Hearing this, the King ordered out his soldiers, who soon captured the Fox and brought him to the palace, where the King sat in state, surrounded by his Wise Men.

"So ho! Master Fox," exclaimed the King, "we have caught you at last."

"So it seems," returned the Fox, calmly. "May I ask your Majesty why I am thus torn from my home, from my wife and children, and brought before you like any common criminal?"

"You have stolen the plum-pudding," answered the King.

"I beg your Majesty's pardon for contradicting you, but I have stolen nothing," declared the Fox. "I can easily prove my innocence. When was the plum-pudding taken?"

"A great deal of it was taken this morning, while the Wise Men slept," said the King.

"Then I can not be the thief," replied the Fox, "as you will admit when you have heard my story."

"Ah! Have you a story to tell?" inquired the King, who dearly loved to hear stories.

"It is a short story, your Majesty; but it will prove clearly that I have not taken your pudding."

"Then tell it," commanded the King. "It is far from my wish to condemn any one who is innocent."

The Wise Men then placed themselves in comfortable positions, and the King crossed his legs and put his hands in his pockets, while the Fox sat before them on his haunches and spoke as follows:

THE FOX'S STORY.

"It has been unusually damp in my den of late, so that both my family and myself have suffered much. First my wife became ill, and then I was afflicted with a bad cold, and in both cases it settled in our throats. Then my four children, who are all of an age, began to complain of sore throats, so that my den became a regular hospital.

"We tried all the medicines we knew of, but they did no good at all. My wife finally begged me to go to consult Doctor

L. Frank Baum

Prairiedog, who lives in a hole in the ground away toward the south. So one morning I said good by to my family and ran swiftly to where the doctor lives.

"Finding no one outside the hole to whom I might apply for admission I walked boldly in, and having followed a long, dark tunnel for some distance, I suddenly came to a door.

"'Come in!' said a voice; so in I walked, and found myself in a very beautiful room, lighted by forty-eight fireflies, which sat in a row on a rail running all around the apartment. In the center of the room was a table, made of clay and painted in bright colors; and seated at this table, with his spectacles on his nose, was the famous Doctor Prairiedog, engaged in eating a dish of stewed snails.

"'Good morning,' said the Doctor; 'will you have some breakfast?'

"'No, thank you,' I replied, for the snails were not to my liking; 'I wish to procure some medicine for my children, who are suffering from sore throats.'

"'How do you know their throats are sore?' inquired the Doctor.

"'It hurts them to swallow,' I explained.

"'Then tell them not to swallow,' said the Doctor, and went on eating.

"'Sir!' I exclaimed, 'if they did not swallow, they would starve to death.'

"'That is true,' remarked the Doctor; 'we must think of something else.' After a moment of silence he cried out: 'Ha! I have it! Go home and cut off their necks, after which you must turn them inside out and hang them on the bushes in the sun. When the necks are thoroughly cured in the sun, turn them right-side-out again and place them on your children's shoulders. Then they will find it does not hurt them to swallow.'

"I thanked the great Doctor and returned home, where I did as he had told me. For the last three days the necks of not only my children but of my wife and myself, as well, have been hanging on the bushes to be cured; so we could not possibly have eaten your plum-pudding. Indeed, it was only an hour ago when I finished putting the neck on the last of my children, and at that moment your soldiers came and arrested me."

When the Fox ceased speaking the King was silent for a while. Then he asked:

"Were the necks all cured?"

"Oh, yes," replied the fox; "the sun cured them nicely."

"You see," remarked the King, turning to his Wise Men; "the Fox has proved his innocence. You were wrong, as usual, in accusing him. I shall now send him home with six baskets of cherry phosphate, as a reward for his honesty. If you have not discovered the thief by the time I return I shall keep my threat and stop your allowance of cake."

Then the Wise Men fell a-trembling, and put their heads together, counseling with one another.

When the King returned, they said: "Your Majesty, it must have been the Bullfrog."

So the King sent his soldiers, who captured the Bullfrog and brought him to the palace.

"Why have you stolen the plum-pudding?" demanded the King, in a stern voice.

"I! Steal your plum-pudding!" exclaimed the Frog, indignantly. "Surely you must be mistaken! I am not at all fond of plum-pudding, and, besides, I have been very busy at home during the past week."

"What have you been doing?" asked the King.

"I will tell you, for then you will know I am innocent of this theft."

So the Bullfrog squatted on a footstool, and, after blinking solemnly at the King and his Wise Men for a moment, spoke as follows:

THE FROG'S STORY.

"Some time ago my wife and I hatched out twelve little tadpoles. They were the sweetest children parents ever looked on. Their heads were all very large and round, and their tails were long and feathery, while their skins were as black and shiny as could be. We were proud of them, my wife and I, and took great pains to train our children properly, that they might become respectable frogs, in time, and be a credit to us.

"We lived in a snug little hole under the bank of the river, and in front of our dwelling was a large stone on which we could sit and watch the baby tadpoles grow. Although they loved best to lie in the mud at the bottom of the river, we knew that exercise is necessary to the proper development of a tadpole; so we decided to teach our youngsters to swim. We divided them into two lots, my wife training six of the children, while I took charge of the other six. We drilled them to swim in single file, in column of twos and in line of battle; but I must acknowledge they were quite stupid, being so young, and, unless we told them when to stop, they would keep on swimming until they bumped themselves into a bank or a stone.

"One day, about a week ago, while teaching our children to swim, we started them all going in single file, one after the other. They swam in a straight line that was very pretty to see, and my wife and I sat on the flat stone and watched them with much pride. Unfortunately at that very moment a large fish swam into our neighborhood and lay on the bottom of the river to rest. It was one of those fishes that hold their great mouths wide open, and I was horrified when I saw the advancing line of tadpoles headed directly toward the gaping mouth of the monster fish. I croaked as loudly as I could for them to stop; but either they failed to hear me, or they would not obey. The next moment all the line of swimming tadpoles had entered the fish's mouth and were lost to our view.

"Mrs. Frog threw herself into my arms with a cry or anguish, exclaiming:

"'Oh, what shall we do? Our children are lost to us forever!'

"'Do not despair,' I answered, although I was myself greatly frightened; 'we must try to prevent the fish from swimming away with our loved ones. If we can keep him here, some way may yet be found to rescue the children.'

"Up to this time the big fish had remained motionless, but there was an expression of surprise in its round eyes, as if it did not know what to make of the lively inhabitants of its stomach.

"Mrs. Frog thought for a moment, and then said:

"'A short distance away is an old fish-line and hook, lying at the bottom of the river, where some boys lost it while fishing one day. If we could only—'

"'Fetch it at once,' I interrupted. 'With its aid we shall endeavor to capture the fish.'

"She hastened away, soon returning with the line, which had a large hook on one end. I tied the other end firmly about the flat stone, and then, advancing cautiously from behind, that

L. Frank Baum

the fish might not see me, I stuck the iron hook through its right gill.

"The monster gave a sudden flop that sent me head over heels a yard away. Then it tried to swim down the stream. But the hook and line held fast, and soon the fish realized it was firmly caught, after which it wisely abandoned the struggle.

"Mrs. Frog and I now sat down to watch the result, and the time of waiting was long and tedious. After several weary days, however, the great fish lay over on its side and expired, and soon after there hopped from its mouth the sweetest little green frog you ever laid eyes on. Another and another followed, until twelve of them stood beside us; and then my wife exclaimed:

"'They are our children, the tadpoles! They have lost their tails and their legs have grown out, but they are our own little ones, nevertheless!'

"Indeed, this was true; for tadpoles always become frogs when a few days old. The children told us they had been quite comfortable inside the great fish, but they were now hungry, for young frogs always have wonderful appetites. So Mrs. Frog and I set to work to feed them, and had just finished this pleasant task when your soldiers came to arrest me. I assure your Majesty this is the first time I have been out of the water for a week. And now, if you will permit me to depart, I will hop back home and see how the youngsters are growing."

When the Bullfrog had ceased speaking the King turned toward the Wise Men and said, angrily:

"It seems you are wrong again, for the Frog is innocent. Your boasted wisdom appears to me very like folly; but I will give you one more chance. If you fail to discover the culprit next time, I shall punish you far more severely than I at first promised."

The King now gave the Bullfrog a present of a red silk necktie, and also sent a bottle of perfumery to Mrs. Frog. The soldiers at once released the prisoner, who joyfully hopped away toward the river.

The Wise Men now rolled their eyes toward the ceiling and twirled their thumbs and thought as hard as they could. At last they told the King they had decided the Yellow Hen was undoubtedly responsible for the theft of the plum-pudding.

So the King sent his soldiers, who searched throughout the Valley and at last captured the Yellow Hen and brought her into the royal presence.

"My Wise Men say you have stolen my plum-pudding," said his Majesty. "If this is true, I am going to punish you severely."

"But it is not true," answered the Yellow Hen; "for I have just returned from a long journey."

"Where have you been?" inquired the King.

"I will tell you," she replied; and, after rearranging a few of her feathers that the rough hands of the soldiers had mussed, the Yellow Hen spoke as follows:

THE YELLOW HEN'S STORY.

"All my life I have been accustomed to hatching out thirteen eggs; but the last time there were only twelve eggs in the nest when I got ready to set. Being experienced in these matters I knew it would never do to set on twelve eggs, so I asked the Red Rooster for his advice.

"He considered the question carefully, and finally told me he had seen a very nice, large egg lying on the rocks near the sugar mountain.

"'If you wish,' said he, 'I will get it for you.'

L. Frank Baum

"'I am very sorry to trouble you, yet certainly I need thirteen eggs,' I answered.

"The Red Rooster is an accommodating fowl, so away he flew, and shortly returned with a large white egg under his wing. This egg I put with the other twelve, and then I set faithfully on my nest for three weeks, at the end of which time I hatched out my chickens.

"Twelve of them were as yellow and fluffy as any mother could wish. But the one that came from the strange egg was black and awkward, and had a large bill and sharp claws. Still thinking he was one of my children, despite his deformity, I gave him as much care as any of them, and soon he outgrew the others and became very big and strong.

"The Red Rooster shook his head, and said, bluntly:

"'That chick will be a great trouble to you, for it looks to me strangely like one of our enemies, the Hawks.'

"'What!' I exclaimed, reproachfully, 'do you think one of my darling children could possibly be a Hawk? I consider that remark almost an insult, Mr. Rooster!'

"The Red Rooster said nothing more; but he kept away from my big, black chick, as if really afraid of it.

"To my great grief this chick suddenly developed a very bad temper, and one day I was obliged to reprove it for grabbing the food away from its brothers. Suddenly it began screaming with anger, and the next moment it sprang on me, digging its sharp claws into my back.

"While I struggled to free myself, he flew far up into the air, carrying me with him, and uttering loud cries that filled me with misgivings. For I now realized, when it was too late, that his voice sounded exactly like the cry of a Hawk!

"Away and away he flew, over mountains, and valleys, and rivers, and lakes, until at last, as I looked down, I saw a man pointing a gun at us. A moment later he shot, and the black chick gave a scream of pain, at the same time releasing his hold of me; so that I fell over and over and finally fluttered to the ground.

"Then I found I had escaped one danger only to encounter another, for as I reached the ground the man seized me and carried me under his arm to his home. Entering the house, he said to his wife:

"'Here is a nice, fat hen for our breakfast.'

"'Put her in the coop,' replied the woman. 'After supper I will cut off her head and pick the feathers from her body.'

"This frightened me greatly, as you may suppose, and when the man placed me in the coop I nearly gave way to despair. But, finding myself alone, I plucked up courage and began looking for a way to escape. To my great joy I soon discovered that one of the slats of the coop was loose, and, having pushed it aside, I was not long in gaining my liberty.

"Once free, I ran away from the place as fast as possible, but did not know in which direction to go, the country being so strange to me. So I fluttered on, half running and half flying, until I reached the place where an army of soldiers was encamped. If these men saw me I feared they would also wish to eat me for breakfast; so I crept into the mouth of a big cannon, thinking I should escape attention and be safe until morning. Soon I fell asleep, and so sound was my slumber that the next thing I heard was the conversation of some soldiers who stood beside the cannon.

"'It is nearly sunrise,' said one. 'You must fire the salute. Is the cannon loaded?'

"'Oh, yes,' answered the other. 'What shall I shoot at?'

L. Frank Baum

"'Fire into the air, for then you will not hurt any one,' said the first soldier.

"By this time I was trembling with fear, and had decided to creep out of the cannon and take the chances of being caught, when, suddenly, 'Bang!' went the big gun, and I shot into the air with a rush like that of a whirlwind.

"The noise nearly deafened me, and my nerves were so shattered that for a time I was helpless. I felt myself go up and up into the air, until soon I was far above the clouds. Then I recovered my wits, and when I began to come down again I tried to fly. I knew the Valley of Mo must be somewhere to the west; so I flew in that direction until I found myself just over the Valley, when I allowed myself to flutter to the ground.

"It seems my troubles were not yet over; for, before I had fully recovered my breath after this long flight, your soldiers seized me and brought me here.

"I am accused of stealing your plum-pudding; but, in truth, your Majesty, I have been away from your kingdom for nine days, and am therefore wholly innocent."

The Yellow Hen had scarce finished this story when the King flew into a violent rage at the deceptions of his Wise Men, and turning to his soldiers he ordered them to arrest the Wise Men and cast them into prison.

Having given the unfortunate Hen a pair of gold earrings that fitted her ears and matched her complexion, the King sent her home with many apologies for having accused her wrongfully.

Then his Majesty seated himself in an easy chair, and pondered how best to punish the foolish Wise Men.

"I would rather have one really Wise Man," he said to himself, "than fifty of these, who pretend to be wise and are not."

That gave him an idea; so the next morning he ordered the Wise Men taken to the royal kitchen, where all were run through the meat chopper until they were ground as fine as mincemeat. Having thoroughly mixed them, the King stirred in a handful of salt, and then made them into one man, which the cook baked in the oven until it was well done.

"Now," said the King, "I have one Wise Man instead of several foolish ones. Perhaps he can tell me who stole the plum-pudding."

"Certainly," replied the Wise Man. "That is quite easy. It was the Purple Dragon."

"Good," cried the monarch; "I have discovered the truth at last!"

And so he had, as you will find by reading the next surprise.

L. Frank Baum

THE FOURTEENTH SURPRISE

THE PUNISHMENT OF THE PURPLE DRAGON

Scarcely had the King spoken when some of his soldiers came running with news that they had seen the Purple Dragon eating plum-pudding in the royal garden.

"What did you do about it?" asked the monarch.

"We did nothing," they answered; "for, had we interfered with its repast, the Dragon would probably have eaten us for dessert."

"That is true," remarked the King. "Yet something must be done to protect us from this monster. For many years it has annoyed us by eating our choicest crops, and nothing we can do seems of any avail to save us from its ravages."

"If we were able to destroy the Dragon," said Prince Thinkabit, "we should be doing our country the greatest possible service."

"We have often tried to destroy it," replied the King, "but the beast always manages to get the best of the fight, having wonderful strength and great cunning. However, let us hold a council of war, and see what is suggested."

So a council of war was called. The Wise Man, all the Princes and Noblemen, the Dog and the Wise Donkey being assembled to talk the matter over.

"I advise that you build a high wall around the Dragon," said the Wise Man. "Then it will be unable to get out, and will starve to death."

"It is strong enough to break down the wall," said the King.

"I suggest you dig a great hole in the ground," remarked the Donkey. "Then the Dragon will fall into it and perish."

"It is too clever to fall into the hole," said the King.

"The best thing to do," declared Timtom, "is to cut off its legs; for then it could not walk into our gardens."

"The scales on its legs are too hard and thick," said the King. "We have tried that, and failed."

"We might take a red-hot iron, and put the Dragon's eyes out," ventured Prince Jollikin.

"Its eyes are glass," replied the King with a sigh, "and the iron would have no effect on them."

"Suppose we tie a tin can to its tail," suggested the Dog. "The rattling of the can would so frighten the Dragon that it would run out of the country."

"Its tail is so long," answered the King, gloomily, "that the Dragon could not hear the can rattle."

Then they all remained silent for a time, thinking so hard that their heads began to ache; but no one seemed able to think of the right thing to do.

Finally the King himself made a proposition.

"One thing we might attempt with some hope of success," said

L. Frank Baum

his Majesty. "Should it fail, we can not be worse off than we are at present. My idea is for us to go in a great body to the castle of the Dragon, and pull out its teeth with a pair of forceps. Having no teeth, the monster will be harmless to annoy us in any way; and, since we seem unable to kill it, I believe this is the best way out of our difficulty."

The King's plan pleased every one, and met with shouts of approval. The council then adjourned, and all the members went to prepare for the fight with the Purple Dragon.

First the blacksmith made a large pair of forceps, to pull the Dragon's teeth with. The handles of the forceps were so long that fifty men could take hold of them at one time. Then the people armed themselves with swords and spears and marched in a great body to the castle of the Purple Dragon.

This remarkable beast, which for so long had kept the Valley of Mo in constant terror, was standing on the front porch of its castle when the army arrived. It looked at the crowd of people in surprise, and said:

"Are you not weary with your attempts to destroy me? What selfish people you must be! Whenever I eat anything that belongs to you, there is a great row, and immediately you come here to fight me. These battles are unpleasant to all of us. The best thing for you to do is to return home and behave yourselves; for I am not in the least afraid of you."

Neither the King nor his people replied to these taunts. They simply brought forward the big pair of forceps and reached them toward the Dragon.

This movement astonished the monster, who, never having been to a dentist in his life, had no idea what the strange instrument was for.

"Surely you can not think to hurt me with that iron thing," it called out, in derision. And then the Dragon laughed at the idea of any one attempting to injure it.

But when the Dragon opened its mouth to laugh, the King opened the jaws of the forceps, quickly closing them again on one of the monster's front teeth.

"Pull!" cried the King; and fifty men seized the handles of the forceps and began to pull with all their strength.

But, pull as they might, the tooth would not come out, and this was the reason: The teeth of Dragons are different from ours, for they go through the jaw and are clinched on the other side. Therefore, no amount of pulling will draw them out.

The King did not know this fact, but thought the tooth must have a long root; so he called again:

"Pull! my brave men; pull!"

And they pulled so hard that the Dragon was nearly pulled from the porch of its castle. To avoid this danger the cunning beast wound the end of its tail around a post of the porch, and tied a hard knot in it.

"Pull!" shouted the King for the third time.

Then a surprising thing happened. Any one who knows anything at all about Dragons is aware that these beasts stretch as easily as if made of india-rubber. Therefore the strong pulling of the fifty men resulted in the Dragon being pulled from its foothold, and, as its tail was fastened to the post, its body began to stretch out.

The King and his people, thinking the tooth was being pulled, started down the hill, the forceps still clinging fast to the monster's big front tooth. And the farther they went the more Dragon's body stretched out.

"Keep going!" cried the King; "we mustn't let go now!" And

away marched the fifty men, and farther and farther stretched the body of the Dragon.

Still holding fast to the forceps, the King and his army marched into the Valley, and away across it, and up the hills on the other side, not even stopping to take breath. When they came to the mountains and the forests, and could go no farther, they looked back; and behold! the Dragon had stretched out so far that it was now no bigger around than a fiddle-string!

"What shall we do now?" asked the fifty men, who were perspiring with the long pull and the march across the Valley.

"I'm sure I don't know," replied the panting King. "Let us tie this end of the beast around a tree. Then we can think what is best to be done."

So they tied that end of the Dragon to a big tree, and sat down to rest, being filled with wonder that the mighty Purple Dragon was now no larger around than a piece of twine.

"The wicked creature will never bother us again," said the King. "Yet it was only by accident we found a way to destroy it. The question now is, what shall we do with this long, thin Dragon? If we leave it here it will trip any one who stumbles against it."

"I shall use it for fiddle-strings," said Prince Fiddlecumdoo, "for the crop failed this year, and I have none for my violin. Let us cut the Dragon up into the proper sizes, and store the strings in the royal warehouse for general use."

The King and the people heartily approved this plan. So the Prince brought a pair of shears and cut the Dragon into equal lengths to use on his violin. Thus the wicked monster was made good use of at last, for the strings had an excellent tone.

And that was not only the end of the Purple Dragon, but there were two other ends of him; one tied to a tree in the mountains and the other fastened to a post of the castle.

That same day the Monarch of Mo gave a magnificent feast to all his people to celebrate the destruction of their greatest foe; and ever afterward the gardens of the Beautiful Valley were free from molestation.

ABOUT THE AUTHOR

Lyman Frank Baum (May 15, 1856–May 6, 1919) was an American author, actor, and independent filmmaker best known as the creator, along with illustrator W. W. Denslow, of one of the most popular books ever written in American children's literature, The Wonderful Wizard of Oz.

Frank was born in Chittenango, New York, into a devout Methodist family of German (father's side) and Scots-Irish (mother's side) origin, the seventh of nine children born to Cynthia Stanton and Benjamin Ward Baum, only five of whom survived into adulthood. He was named "Lyman" after his father's brother, but always disliked this name, and preferred to go by "Frank". His mother, Cynthia Stanton, was a direct descendant of Thomas Stanton, one of the four Founders of what is now Stonington, Connecticut.

Frank started writing at an early age, perhaps due to an early fascination with printing. His father bought him a cheap printing press, and Frank used it to produce The Rose Lawn Home Journal with the help of his younger brother, Harry Clay Baum, with whom he had always been close.

In 1900, Baum and Denslow (with whom he shared the copyright) published The Wonderful Wizard of Oz to much critical and financial acclaim. The book was the best-selling children's book for two years after its initial publication. Baum went on to write thirteen other novels based on the places and people of the Land of Oz.

His final Oz book, Glinda of Oz was published a year after his death in 1920 but the Oz series was continued long after his death by other authors, notably Ruth Plumly Thompson, who wrote an additional nineteen Oz books.

Baum made use of several pseudonyms for some of his other, non-Oz books. They include:

Edith Van Dyne (the Aunt Jane's Nieces series), Laura Bancroft (Twinkle and Chubbins, Policeman Bluejay), Floyd Akers (The Boy Fortune Hunters series, continuing the Sam Steele series), Suzanne Metcalf (Annabel), Schuyler Staunton (The Fate of a Crown, Daughters of Destiny), John Estes Cooke (Tamawaca Folks), Capt. Hugh Fitzgerald (the Sam Steele series), Baum also anonymously wrote The Last Egyptian: A Romance of the Nile.

Baum died on May 6, 1919, aged 62, and was buried in the Forest Lawn Memorial Park Cemetery, in Glendale, California.

Choose from Thousands of 1stWorldLibrary Classics By

A. M. Barnard
Ada Leverson
Adolphus William Ward
Aesop
Agatha Christie
Alexander Aaronsohn
Alexander Kielland
Alexandre Dumas
Alfred Gatty
Alfred Ollivant
Alice Duer Miller
Alice Turner Curtis
Alice Dunbar
Allen Chapman
Alleyne Ireland
Ambrose Bierce
Amelia E. Barr
Amory H. Bradford
Andrew Lang
Andrew McFarland Davis
Andy Adams
Angela Brazil
Anna Alice Chapin
Anna Sewell
Annie Besant
Annie Hamilton Donnell
Annie Payson Call
Annie Roe Carr
Annonaymous
Anton Chekhov
Archibald Lee Fletcher
Arnold Bennett
Arthur C. Benson
Arthur Conan Doyle
Arthur M. Winfield
Arthur Ransome
Arthur Schnitzler
Arthur Train
Atticus
B.H. Baden-Powell
B. M. Bower
B. C. Chatterjee
Baroness Emmuska Orczy
Baroness Orczy
Basil King
Bayard Taylor
Ben Macomber
Bertha Muzzy Bower
Bjornstjerne Bjornson

Booth Tarkington
Boyd Cable
Bram Stoker
C. Collodi
C. E. Orr
C. M. Ingleby
Carolyn Wells
Catherine Parr Traill
Charles A. Eastman
Charles Amory Beach
Charles Dickens
Charles Dudley Warner
Charles Farrar Browne
Charles Ives
Charles Kingsley
Charles Klein
Charles Hanson Towne
Charles Lathrop Pack
Charles Romyn Dake
Charles Whibley
Charles Willing Beale
Charlotte M. Braeme
Charlotte M. Yonge
Charlotte Perkins Stetson
Clair W. Hayes
Clarence Day Jr.
Clarence E. Mulford
Clemence Housman
Confucius
Coningsby Dawson
Cornelis DeWitt Wilcox
Cyril Burleigh
D. H. Lawrence
Daniel Defoe
David Garnett
Dinah Craik
Don Carlos Janes
Donald Keyhoe
Dorothy Kilner
Dougan Clark
Douglas Fairbanks
E. Nesbit
E. P. Roe
E. Phillips Oppenheim
E. S. Brooks
Earl Barnes
Edgar Rice Burroughs
Edith Van Dyne
Edith Wharton

Edward Everett Hale
Edward J. O'Biren
Edward S. Ellis
Edwin L. Arnold
Eleanor Atkins
Eleanor Hallowell Abbott
Eliot Gregory
Elizabeth Gaskell
Elizabeth McCracken
Elizabeth Von Arnim
Ellem Key
Emerson Hough
Emilie F. Carlen
Emily Bronte
Emily Dickinson
Enid Bagnold
Enilor Macartney Lane
Erasmus W. Jones
Ernie Howard Pie
Ethel May Dell
Ethel Turner
Ethel Watts Mumford
Eugene Sue
Eugenie Foa
Eugene Wood
Eustace Hale Ball
Evelyn Everett-green
Everard Cotes
F. H. Cheley
F. J. Cross
F. Marion Crawford
Fannie E. Newberry
Federick Austin Ogg
Ferdinand Ossendowski
Fergus Hume
Florence A. Kilpatrick
Fremont B. Deering
Francis Bacon
Francis Darwin
Frances Hodgson Burnett
Frances Parkinson Keyes
Frank Gee Patchin
Frank Harris
Frank Jewett Mather
Frank L. Packard
Frank V. Webster
Frederic Stewart Isham
Frederick Trevor Hill
Frederick Winslow Taylor

Friedrich Kerst
Friedrich Nietzsche
Fyodor Dostoyevsky
G.A. Henty
G.K. Chesterton
Gabrielle E. Jackson
Garrett P. Serviss
Gaston Leroux
George A. Warren
George Ade
Geroge Bernard Shaw
George Cary Eggleston
George Durston
George Ebers
George Eliot
George Gissing
George MacDonald
George Meredith
George Orwell
George Sylvester Viereck
George Tucker
George W. Cable
George Wharton James
Gertrude Atherton
Gordon Casserly
Grace E. King
Grace Gallatin
Grace Greenwood
Grant Allen
Guillermo A. Sherwell
Gulielma Zollinger
Gustav Flaubert
H. A. Cody
H. B. Irving
H.C. Bailey
H. G. Wells
H. H. Munro
H. Irving Hancock
H. R. Naylor
H. Rider Haggard
H. W. C. Davis
Haldeman Julius
Hall Caine
Hamilton Wright Mabie
Hans Christian Andersen
Harold Avery
Harold McGrath
Harriet Beecher Stowe
Harry Castlemon
Harry Coghill
Harry Houidini

Hayden Carruth
Helent Hunt Jackson
Helen Nicolay
Hendrik Conscience
Hendy David Thoreau
Henri Barbusse
Henrik Ibsen
Henry Adams
Henry Ford
Henry Frost
Henry James
Henry Jones Ford
Henry Seton Merriman
Henry W Longfellow
Herbert A. Giles
Herbert Carter
Herbert N. Casson
Herman Hesse
Hildegard G. Frey
Homer
Honore De Balzac
Horace B. Day
Horace Walpole
Horatio Alger Jr.
Howard Pyle
Howard R. Garis
Hugh Lofting
Hugh Walpole
Humphry Ward
Ian Maclaren
Inez Haynes Gillmore
Irving Bacheller
Isabel Cecilia Williams
Isabel Hornibrook
Israel Abrahams
Ivan Turgenev
J.G.Austin
J. Henri Fabre
J. M. Barrie
J. M. Walsh
J. Macdonald Oxley
J. R. Miller
J. S. Fletcher
J. S. Knowles
J. Storer Clouston
J. W. Duffield
Jack London
Jacob Abbott
James Allen
James Andrews
James Baldwin

James Branch Cabell
James DeMille
James Joyce
James Lane Allen
James Lane Allen
James Oliver Curwood
James Oppenheim
James Otis
James R. Driscoll
Jane Abbott
Jane Austen
Jane L. Stewart
Janet Aldridge
Jens Peter Jacobsen
Jerome K. Jerome
Jessie Graham Flower
John Buchan
John Burroughs
John Cournos
John F. Kennedy
John Gay
John Glasworthy
John Habberton
John Joy Bell
John Kendrick Bangs
John Milton
John Philip Sousa
John Taintor Foote
Jonas Lauritz Idemil Lie
Jonathan Swift
Joseph A. Altsheler
Joseph Carey
Joseph Conrad
Joseph E. Badger Jr
Joseph Hergesheimer
Joseph Jacobs
Jules Vernes
Julian Hawthrone
Julie A Lippmann
Justin Huntly McCarthy
Kakuzo Okakura
Karle Wilson Baker
Kate Chopin
Kenneth Grahame
Kenneth McGaffey
Kate Langley Bosher
Kate Langley Bosher
Katherine Cecil Thurston
Katherine Stokes
L. A. Abbot
L. T. Meade

L. Frank Baum
Latta Griswold
Laura Dent Crane
Laura Lee Hope
Laurence Housman
Lawrence Beasley
Leo Tolstoy
Leonid Andreyev
Lewis Carroll
Lewis Sperry Chafer
Lilian Bell
Lloyd Osbourne
Louis Hughes
Louis Joseph Vance
Louis Tracy
Louisa May Alcott
Lucy Fitch Perkins
Lucy Maud Montgomery
Luther Benson
Lydia Miller Middleton
Lyndon Orr
M. Corvus
M. H. Adams
Margaret E. Sangster
Margret Howth
Margaret Vandercook
Margaret W. Hungerford
Margret Penrose
Maria Edgeworth
Maria Thompson Daviess
Mariano Azuela
Marion Polk Angellotti
Mark Overton
Mark Twain
Mary Austin
Mary Catherine Crowley
Mary Cole
Mary Hastings Bradley
Mary Roberts Rinehart
Mary Rowlandson
M. Wollstonecraft Shelley
Maud Lindsay
Max Beerbohm
Myra Kelly
Nathaniel Hawthrone
Nicolo Machiavelli
O. F. Walton
Oscar Wilde

Owen Johnson
P.G. Wodehouse
Paul and Mabel Thorne
Paul G. Tomlinson
Paul Severing
Percy Brebner
Percy Keese Fitzhugh
Peter B. Kyne
Plato
Quincy Allen
R. Derby Holmes
R. L. Stevenson
R. S. Ball
Rabindranath Tagore
Rahul Alvares
Ralph Bonehill
Ralph Henry Barbour
Ralph Victor
Ralph Waldo Emmerson
Rene Descartes
Ray Cummings
Rex Beach
Rex E. Beach
Richard Harding Davis
Richard Jefferies
Richard Le Gallienne
Robert Barr
Robert Frost
Robert Gordon Anderson
Robert L. Drake
Robert Lansing
Robert Lynd
Robert Michael Ballantyne
Robert W. Chambers
Rosa Nouchette Carey
Rudyard Kipling
Saint Augustine
Samuel B. Allison
Samuel Hopkins Adams
Sarah Bernhardt
Sarah C. Hallowell
Selma Lagerlof
Sherwood Anderson
Sigmund Freud
Standish O'Grady
Stanley Weyman
Stella Benson
Stella M. Francis

Stephen Crane
Stewart Edward White
Stijn Streuvels
Swami Abhedananda
Swami Parmananda
T. S. Ackland
T. S. Arthur
The Princess Der Ling
Thomas A. Janvier
Thomas A Kempis
Thomas Anderton
Thomas Bailey Aldrich
Thomas Bulfinch
Thomas De Quincey
Thomas Dixon
Thomas H. Huxley
Thomas Hardy
Thomas More
Thornton W. Burgess
U. S. Grant
Upton Sinclair
Valentine Williams
Various Authors
Vaughan Kester
Victor Appleton
Victor G. Durham
Victoria Cross
Virginia Woolf
Wadsworth Camp
Walter Camp
Walter Scott
Washington Irving
Wilbur Lawton
Wilkie Collins
Willa Cather
Willard F. Baker
William Dean Howells
William le Queux
W. Makepeace Thackeray
William W. Walter
William Shakespeare
Winston Churchill
Yei Theodora Ozaki
Yogi Ramacharaka
Young E. Allison
Zane Grey

Printed in the United States
83635LV00006B/1/A